Our I
of Fatima

Paul De Marco

ISBN : 9798744019709

- Contents -

- Introduction -

In the spring of 1915, Europe was embroiled in the horror of World War I and the ferocious Battle of Gallipoli had just begun. Unlike in previous wars, innocent civilians found themselves as targets too, and a shocking example of this was the sinking of the cruise liner Lusitania twelve miles off the Irish coast on 7th May of that year which claimed 1198 lives. However, the tiny village of Aljustrel in the parish of Fatima in Portugal was largely untouched by the war and the town had absolutely no claim to fame at that time. But events in this sleepy farming village over the next two years were about to rock the Catholic Church and have a profound effect on world history.

Three young children claimed that they'd seen a vision of the Virgin Mary on the **13th of May 1917** at a place named the Cova da Iria, and they said that she had asked them to return there on the 13th of each month over the next six months. During this period, the children were given various secrets as well as a terrifying **vision of Hell**, but the secrets were only made public many years later. Our Lady assured the children that World War I would soon end but she warned that unless mankind repented and turned from sin then a more devastating war would break out during the pontificate of Pius XI.

She called for the pope, in conjunction with all the bishops of the Church, to consecrate Russia to her, and Our Lady also asked for a devotion to be made in reparation for the sins against her Immaculate Heart. She promised to be present at the time of death of all those who made this First Five Saturdays devotion with the graces necessary for their salvation. Our Lady gave an assurance that if these requests were met, then the world would enjoy peace and Russia would be converted. If not, then mankind would again experience war and Russia would spread her errors throughout the world. She said that the sign that this chastisement was imminent would be 'a night illumined by an unknown light.'

The disbelieving villagers and priests made life difficult for Lucia and her cousins, Francisco and Jacinta, and even their own parents thought that they were lying. However the visions continued and the children astounded the villagers by saying that Our Lady would give a sign on the 13th of October 1917 for all to see and believe. A massive crowd estimated at 70,000 descended on the Cova da Iria that day and stood there in the mud and the driving rain. Simple farmers, journalists, scientists, believers and non-believers alike were left stunned by what they saw - the **Miracle of the Sun**. Yet despite this astonishing sign, the Church and the wider world were slow to respond and there was indeed a night illumined by an unknown light on the **25th of January 1938** which was visible throughout the whole of Europe. Just six weeks later, Germany annexed Austria and mankind was on the road to a war which would claim 85 million lives and our history books show us the effect that Russian imperialism subsequently had on the world.

Francisco died in 1919 aged ten, and Jacinta died at the age of nine the following year, both victims of the Spanish Flu outbreak which killed at least 3% of the global population. However, Lucia survived and she played a pivotal role in sharing the message of Fatima with the world throughout her entire life. Lucia committed the text of the third secret to writing on the 9th of January 1944 and placed it in a sealed envelope which was ultimately taken to the Vatican thirteen years later on the 16th of April 1957. Here it lay unopened in a little wooden chest in the office of Pope Pius XII, and even the subsequent popes, John XXIII and Paul VI both read the secret but would not make it public.

On **13th May 1981**, the anniversary date of the first apparition in 1917, there was an assassination attempt on John Paul II as he was being driven slowly through the crowds gathered in St Peter's Square. The Pope was convinced that Our Lady had intervened to save his life and so he requested all the documentation on the apparitions at Fatima and later consecrated Russia to the Immaculate Heart of Mary on the 25th of March 1984. Since then, the world has witnessed the collapse of the Soviet Union which began with the dismantling of the Berlin wall on 9th November 1989. One of the bullets which so nearly took the Pope's life is now set in the crown of the statue of Our Lady of Fatima. Eventually, the text of the third secret and an interpretation of it were made public on the **26th of June 2000**, some 83 years after Lucia had witnessed the vision, and this caused massive controversy.

This book gives a fascinating account of the story of Fatima, from the very first apparitions of an angel in 1915, through to the present day, all set in the context of World history. It looks at the response of the Church and at the timeless message that Our Lady gave to the children, which is every bit as relevant today as it was back in 1917.

- Chapter 1 -

An angel prepares the way

Lucia dos Santos was born to her parents, Antonio and Maria Rosa on the 22nd of March 1907 and she was the youngest of seven children. The family had a few plots of land on which they farmed vegetables and they also owned a small flock of sheep, with one of her sisters helping to support the family by working as a weaver and another as a seamstress, both working from home.

The residents of Aljustrel were mainly farmers and the town is located about 75 kilometres south of Coimbra and 120 kilometres north of Lisbon and still only had a population of below 10,000 in 2011.

Lucia was baptised when she was eight days old, and her mother ensured that she, along with her other children, were raised in the Catholic faith. Maria was happy to let some of the other mothers bring their young children to her house so that they could go off to work, and so Lucia was always surrounded with other youngsters from an early age. They were happy days, and she was particularly fond of her cousins, Francisco and Jacinta Marto who lived just two houses away.

Francisco was about 14 months younger than Lucia, and Jacinta was three years younger than her, but the cousins had very different personalities with Jacinta being outgoing and effervescent whereas Francisco was quiet, calm and rather submissive in nature. They would meet up daily to play their favourite games together, using buttons or small stones as forfeits with Jacinta typically winning Lucia's buttons, which meant that she had to remove them from her clothes and risk a scolding from her mother. But fortunately her sisters were usually around to stitch them back on before her mum found out about it.

The village held regular dances and festivals, and Lucia and Jacinta both loved to dance whereas Francisco preferred to just play his flute and to watch all the celebrations from a distance. At Carnival time, everyone would be involved in preparing food for the banquet, in making costumes and dancing, and the festivities would go on well into the night for three whole days.

Maria gave catechism lessons to her own children, but often Jacinta and Francisco joined in, along with the youngsters from other local families. It was customary for the children to first receive Holy Communion at the age of ten and only after the parish priest was satisfied that the child had a reasonable understanding of their faith. However, Maria's lessons paid dividends and the young Lucia was allowed to make her First Communion at the age of just six.

The following year, Lucia was given responsibility for taking the sheep out to find pasture on the slopes of the hillsides nearby. Her sister, Carolina had been doing this up until then, but as she was now twelve years old, Maria Rosa felt that it was time that she went out to work. Lucia soon befriended three other children who were looking after flocks of sheep of their own and so she spent many days in their company. One was a girl named Teresa Matias, the other, Teresa's sister, Maria Rosa, and the third was a girl named Maria Justino.

Lucia was unsure of the exact date but it was certainly in 1915 when she witnessed an apparition of an angel for the very first time. She and her friends had led their flocks high up onto a hillside known as the Cabeco and from this vantage point they had a beautiful view of the tree-covered valley below them.

At around midday, they sat down to eat their pack lunches as they gazed down at the sheep, and once finished they began to pray the rosary together, something that was customary to do in Portugal at that time. It was then that Lucia and her friends suddenly saw a vision of an illuminated figure of human form but lacking any distinctive features that was suspended above tree level. She described the apparition as resembling a statue made of snow which was almost transparent, and they were mesmerised by this sight, watching it intently until the figure finally disappeared from view.

Lucia's three companions rushed home to tell their families about the apparition and although Lucia had decided to keep quiet about the whole affair, news of this soon got back to her mother. But Maria Rosa was completely dismissive of the alleged supernatural sighting, saying that it was all just 'Childish nonsense!'

Lucia later said that the vision had looked like a person wrapped up in a sheet suspended in the air, and so she was teased mercilessly for this by all the villagers including her own sisters. However these four children witnessed the apparition on two further occasions on the very same hillside and again it seemed to have no discernible features, nor did it speak to them. After each of these events, her friends once again told their families about what they'd seen and when her neighbours reported this back to Maria Rosa she was absolutely furious and gave Lucia a scolding for talking rubbish once again.

Jacinta couldn't wait for her older cousin, Lucia to return each day from the Cabeco, and as soon as she heard the tinkling noise of the bells on the sheep she would come running over to meet her. Shortly after the third apparition, Francisco and Jacinta were allowed to start taking their own sheep out to pasture and so Lucia opted to leave her three girl friends so that she could spend time with the cousins instead.

There was some land in the foothills of the eastern slope of the Cabeco that Lucia's family owned called Chousa Velha, and one day in the spring of 1916 the trio led their flocks out to pasture there. It began to rain, and so they walked higher up on the hillside to take shelter under an overhanging boulder which was in an olive grove. After their snack lunch they said the customary rosary, but instead of saying the full prayers they abbreviated them to just saying 'Our Father' and 'Hail Mary' on the beads so that they could quickly get back to their games.

By now the rain had eased off, the air was calm and the sun was shining brightly, but from out of nowhere a strong wind suddenly began to blow which violently shook the trees and startled them. Then, as they gazed up at the sky above the olive trees they were shocked to see an apparition in the distance that was coming towards them.

The children were too shocked to speak as they watched this strange sight which Lucia described as having been dazzlingly bright and transparent like crystal when strong sunlight shines through it. As the apparition came closer, they could discern its features better and they saw that it had the appearance of a young man around the age of fourteen or fifteen.

The apparition drew closer and then said, "Do not be afraid! I am the Angel of Peace. Pray with me."

The angel bowed down until his head touched the ground and then asked them to repeat a prayer which he recited with them three times over:

"My God, I believe, I adore, I hope and I love you! I ask pardon of You for those who do not believe, do not adore, do not hope, and do not love You."

The angel also said, **"Pray thus. The hearts of Jesus and Mary are attentive to the voice of your supplications."**

The angel then vanished from their sight but the three children remained on their knees repeating this prayer over and over again, and the whole experience was so intense and mesmerising that the children were unable to speak to each other. The 'spiritual atmosphere' as Lucia described it, was still felt by the children the next day and it only gradually faded away with time.

Lucia and Jacinta could both hear what the angel had said, but for some reason Francisco could only see the angel and hear what Lucia was saying in response to him. Understandably, the shock of this apparition and what the angel had said had a profound effect on them and so they spent a lot of time in the fields kneeling down and saying the prayer that had been given to them.

Later that year, during the summer of 1916, Lucia and her cousins Jacinta and Francisco again saw the angel but this time it was while they were playing by a well at the bottom of the garden belonging to her parents. During the summer, the children would typically bring the sheep back from the hillside before midday so as to avoid the intense heat and they would find some shade under the trees by this well.

The angel said to them, **"What are you doing? Pray, pray very much! The most holy Hearts of Jesus and Mary have designs of mercy on you. Make of everything you can a sacrifice, and offer it to God as an act of reparation for the sins by which He is offended, and in supplication for the conversion of sinners. You will thus draw down peace upon your country. I am its Angel Guardian, the Angel of Portugal. Above all, accept and bear with submission the suffering which the Lord will send you."**

This is how Lucia later described the words of the angel:

"They were like a light which made us understand who God is, how He loves us and desires to be loved; the value of sacrifice, how pleasing it is to Him and how, on account of it, He grants the grace of conversion to sinners."

Once again, Francisco was unable to hear the angel speak, but he could hear what Lucia was saying during the apparition. At Cabeco, the angel had announced himself as the Angel of Peace, and so it's uncertain whether this angel and the Angel of Portugal were one and the same, but Lucia always believed that the apparitions were of the same angel.

This time, the three children somehow managed to keep these apparitions to themselves to avoid being ridiculed by the other children, their parents and many of the adults in the village.

After the apparition, Jacinta said, "I don't know how I feel. I can no longer talk, or sing, or play. I haven't strength enough for anything."

Francisco replied, "Neither have I. But what of it? The angel is more beautiful than all of this. Let's think about him."

A few months later, in late September or early October, they were again at the Cabeco at their hide-out under the overhanging rock with their heads to the ground saying the prayer that the angel had previously given them. They were suddenly immersed in a supernatural light, and raising their heads they again saw the angel standing right there in front of them. This time, he held a chalice in his left hand and above the chalice suspended in mid air was a host like the ones they saw at mass, and the children watched as drops of blood fell from the host into the chalice. The angel then let the chalice go, which was left suspended in the air by itself with the host above it, before he knelt down with the children to pray.

He asked them to recite this prayer three times:

"Most Holy Trinity, Father, Son and Holy Spirit, I adore You profoundly and offer You the most precious Body, Blood, Soul and Divinity of Jesus Christ, present in all the tabernacles of the world, in reparation for the outrages, sacrileges and indifference with which He Himself is offended. And, through the infinite merits of His most Sacred Heart, and the Immaculate Heart of Mary, I beg of You the conversion of poor sinners."

After Lucia and her cousins had recited this prayer three times, the angel stood up and took the host in one hand and the Chalice in the other. He placed the host on Lucia's tongue and then gave the blood from the chalice to both Jacinta and Francisco.

The angel said, **"Eat and drink the Body and Blood of Jesus Christ, horribly outraged by ungrateful men. Make reparation for their crimes and console your God."**

The angel then prostrated himself on the ground and repeated the prayer he had taught them another three times over with the children. At this point the angel then vanished but the children remained for several hours with their heads to the ground reciting the new prayer.

In her memoirs, Lucia wrote: "the force of the presence of God was so intense that it absorbed us and almost completely annihilated us. It seemed to deprive us even of the use of our bodily senses for a considerable length of time."

For several days after this apparition, Francisco felt unable to speak, but he later said, "I love to see the Angel, but the worst of it is that, afterwards, we are unable to do anything. I couldn't even walk. I don't know what was the matter with me."

He also said to Lucia: "The Angel gave you Holy Communion, but what was it that he gave to Jacinta and me?"

It was young Jacinta who answered, saying, "It was Holy Communion, too. Didn't you see that it was the Blood that fell from the Host?"

He replied, "I felt that God was within me, but I did not know how!"

The angel's prayer is very similar to the one that Jesus gave to Sister Maria Faustina of the Sisters of Our Lady of Mercy when he appeared to her in her convent at Vilnius on 13th and 14th September 1935:

'Eternal Father, I offer You the Body and Blood, Soul and Divinity of Your dearly beloved Son, our Lord Jesus Christ, in atonement for our sins and those of the whole world.'

There's more detail about Sister Faustina and the Chaplet of Divine Mercy prayers in chapter 13, which covers the subject of Hell.

This was the last time that the angel appeared to Lucia, Jacinta and Francisco, but now visitations by the angel would give way to apparitions by the Virgin Mary herself.

- Chapter 2 -
Apparitions of Our Lady

By this time, Lucia's mother had sent all her daughters out to work and so the house was much quieter than usual as during the day it was only Lucia, her brother and her mother who were at home until her father arrived back from work. Lucia was still looking after the sheep, and her brother was taking care of the vegetables and olive trees on the small plots of land the family owned. In common with most parents, Maria didn't adjust too well to the sudden quiet in the house and she frequently burst into tears because she missed her children so much.

Her mother's unhappiness upset Lucia greatly and so she would often leave the house and wander down to the well to have a cry herself, and Lucia's cousins would sometimes meet her down there, with Jacinta always showing her natural empathy. The little seven-year-old would put her arm around Lucia to comfort her and she would innocently say, **"My God, it is as an act of reparation, and for the conversion of sinners, that we offer You all these sufferings and sacrifices."**

Jacinta often gave her lunch to the poor children that she encountered on the way to pasture the sheep and in many other little ways she kept true to the request of the angel that she should offer her trials and difficulties up as a sacrifice to God. Lucia recalled in her memoirs that her mother became seriously ill about the time of the first apparition of Our Lady to the children in May 1917.

1st apparition: 13th May 1917

On the morning of Sunday 13th May 1917, Lucia and her cousins led their sheep to an area just north of Aljustrel for them to find pasture. This land belonged to Lucia's father, and was called Cova da Iria, or peaceful hollow. (The 13th of May is a significant date in the Church as it is the Feast of Our Lady of the Blessed Sacrament.)

This was a time of tremendous destruction and fear in Europe, as World War 1 had been raging for almost three years by now. By this time, millions had died at the battles of Mons, Ypres, Gallipoli, Loos, Verdun and the Somme. The casualty rates were unprecedented in warfare and an example of this is that Britain suffered 57,470 casualties, of which 19,240 died on the first day of the Battle of the Somme alone. America had declared war on Germany on 6th April 1917, the month before the first apparition.

In the fields around the Cova da Iria, about two kilometers from Aljustrel, there was complete tranquility as Lucia, her cousins and a few dozen sheep arrived. As the animals grazed, the children climbed higher up the hillside and they were all playing together when they saw a brilliant flash of light. Although the sky was cloudless, they thought that it could have been lightning and so they decided to take the sheep home with them. They'd moved the flock about half way down the slope when they suddenly saw a second bright flash of light in the sky.

It was then that they witnessed an apparition of a dazzlingly-bright lady dressed completely in white. She appeared to be standing on top of a small Holm Oak (Holly Oak) sapling which was about a metre high. As with the vision of the angel, she radiated an intensely brilliant light, far brighter than that of the sun. Lucia described her as follows: **"She was more brilliant than the sun and radiated a light clearer and more intense than a crystal glass filled with sparkling water, when the rays of the burning sun shine through it."**

The children were astounded at this apparition, which was only a few feet in front of them and they just stood there immersed in the brilliant light which radiated from her. The ten-year-old Lucia was unafraid of this vision and later recalled that she had felt peace, joy and happiness in her presence. In some ways this was the same emotion that she'd felt in the presence of the angel but on those occasions the children had felt an impulse to fall to the ground and they'd found it difficult to move or even to talk. In the presence of the lady, Lucia felt great exultation and she also felt relaxed in speaking to her.

The lady simply said, "Do not be afraid. I will do you no harm."

Lucia then innocently asked her, "Where are you from?" to which the lady replied, "I am from heaven."

Lucia then said, "What do you want of me?"

To this the lady replied, "I have come to ask you to come here for six months in succession, on the 13th day, at this same hour. Later on, I will tell you who I am and what I want. Afterwards I will return here yet a seventh time."

Lucia then asked, "Shall I go to Heaven too?"

She replied, "Yes, you will."

Then Lucia said, "And Jacinta?"

The lady replied, "She will go also."

Finally Lucia asked, "And Francisco?" to which she replied, "He will go there too, but he must say many rosaries."

Lucia then plucked up the courage to ask about two other people who had recently died. One was a young woman named Maria, who had died at the age of sixteen, and the other was a woman named Amelia, who had died when she was about eighteen to twenty years-of-age. These girls had frequently visited her house to be taught how to weave.

Lucia asked, "Is Maria das Neves in Heaven?"

The lady then replied, "Yes, she is."

Then she said, "And Amelia?"

To this, the lady said, "She will be in purgatory until the end of the world."

(Her reference to purgatory is highly significant as this subject is rarely covered by priests in their homilies today. It's as though purgatory has been quietly dropped from the teachings of the Catholic Church, and this topic is covered later in the book.)

The Lady then asked the children, "Are you willing to offer yourselves to God and bear all the sufferings He wills to send you, as an act of reparation for the sins by which He is offended, and of supplication for the conversion of sinners?"

To this they bravely replied, "Yes, we are willing!"

The lady then said, "Then you are going to have much to suffer, but the grace of God will be your comfort."

Lucia said that as the lady spoke these words, she opened her hands and transmitted an intense, penetrating light from them. It seems that it was through this light that she communicated with the children in a special way. Lucia described it as follows:

"Our Lady opened her hands for the first time, communicating to us a light so intense that, as it streamed from her hands, its rays penetrated our hearts and the innermost depths of our souls, making us see ourselves in God, who was that light, more clearly than we see ourselves in the best of mirrors. Then, moved by an interior impulse that was also communicated to us, we fell on our knees, repeating in our hearts, 'O most Holy Trinity, I adore You! My God, my God, I love you in the most Blessed Sacrament!'"

Before she departed, Our Lady said, **"Pray the rosary every day, in order to obtain peace for the world, and the end of the war."**

(Her statement here clearly shows the powerful effect that prayer can have on events unfolding in our world and the book later shows how the outcomes of prophecies can be radically altered too.)

After saying this, the children saw Our Lady slowly rise up into the air in an easterly direction with a light surrounding her that also preceded the direction of her movement until she finally disappeared from view. Again all three children saw the apparition of Our lady but Francisco was unable to hear what she had actually said. When Lucia told him that she had said that he would go to Heaven, he was overjoyed and said, "Oh my dear Our Lady! I'll say as many rosaries as you want!"

Francisco was very diligent in praying the rosary from then on and would often be in prayer while Lucia and Jacinta played together. Lucia recalled him saying one day: "I loved seeing the Angel, but I loved still more seeing Our Lady. What I loved most of all was to see Our Lord in that light from Our Lady which penetrated our hearts. I love God so much! But He is very sad because of so many sins! We must never commit any sins again."

After this visitation by Our Lady, Jacinta was unable to keep the experience to herself, and so she told her parents what had happened. News spread very quickly throughout the town about Jacinta's claim to have seen Our Lady, and this caused problems for the children, as their parents still thought that they'd just made the whole story up. As more and more people heard of the apparition, there was increasing pressure on Maria Rosa to get Lucia to admit that she'd just lied about the vision and even Lucia's sisters joined in the verbal abuse against her.

2nd apparition: 13th June

This was the feast day of Saint Anthony, the patron saint of Portugal, and this event was widely celebrated throughout the country at that time, with villagers dressing up for the occasion and holding a dance afterwards. But instead of joining their families in the public celebrations, Lucia and her cousins had decided to return to the Cova da Iria in the hope of seeing Our Lady once again.

Lucia took the sheep out to pasture at the crack of dawn and had intended to bring them home in time for her to attend mass at 10am. However, Lucia's brother ran out to find her on the hillside, telling her to come home straight away as several people from the surrounding villages had arrived outside their house and wanted to see her. These strangers asked if they could accompany Lucia to the Cova da Iria later, to which Lucia agreed, but she first attended the 8am mass.

The sight of all these strangers waiting outside her house infuriated Maria Rosa who became even more determined to get her daughter to confess that she'd been lying all along. This was a very difficult time for Lucia and she was frequently found in tears by Jacinta who would then try to console her. She would say, "Don't cry. Surely, these are the sacrifices which the Angel said that God was going to send us. That's why you are suffering, so that you can make reparation to Him and convert sinners."

When they arrived at the Cova, the children began praying the rosary and by now there were a few dozen people from the surrounding villages standing there with them. As soon as they'd finished praying, they once again saw bright flashes of light approaching and then Lucia, Francisco and Jacinta saw Our Lady standing above the oak sapling nearby, just as she had done on 13th May.

It had been a whole month since the children had first seen the Virgin Mary, and in that time they had planned what they would say should they ever see her again.

Lucia asked, "What do you want of me?"

Our Lady answered, "I wish you to come here on the 13th of next month, to pray the rosary every day, and to learn to read. Later I will tell you what I want."

Lucia then mentioned someone who was ill, and she asked if he could be healed, to which Our Lady replied, "If he is converted he will be cured during the year."

Lucia then said, "I would like to ask you to take us to heaven."

Our Lady answered, "Yes. I will take Jacinta and Francisco soon. But you are to stay here some time longer. Jesus wishes to make use of you to make me known and loved. **He wants to establish in the world devotion to my Immaculate Heart. I promise salvation to those who embrace it, and those souls will be loved by God like flowers placed by me to adorn his throne**."

(This promise refers to the Devotion of the First Five Saturdays, which Our Lady would later explain to Lucia on 10th December 1925.)

Lucia then asked, "Am I to stay here alone?"

Our lady replied, No my daughter. Are you suffering a great deal? Don't lose heart. I will never forsake you. My Immaculate Heart will be your refuge and the way that will lead you to God."

After this, Our Lady opened her hands and immersed the children in an intensely bright light. Lucia noticed that Jacinta and Francisco were in the part of the light which rose upwards towards Heaven, but that she was in a section of light that shone down towards the Earth. The children said that it felt as though they were immersed in God's love.

Lucia also described seeing something else in this encounter:

"In front of the palm of Our Lady's right hand was a Heart encircled by thorns which pierced it. We understood that this was the Immaculate Heart of Mary, outraged by the sins of humanity, and seeking reparation."

Again, Francisco was unable to hear Our Lady speak, and he asked Lucia, "Why did Our Lady have a Heart in her hand, spreading out over the world that great light which is God? You were with Our Lady in the light which went down towards the earth, and Jacinta was with me in the light which rose towards heaven!"

Lucia replied, "That is because you and Jacinta will soon go to heaven while I, with the Immaculate Heart of Mary, will remain for some time longer on earth."

Francisco then said, "How many years longer will you stay here?" to which Lucia replied, "I don't know. Quite a lot."

Francisco then asked, "Was it Our Lady who said so?" and Lucia replied, "Yes, and I saw it in the light that shone into our hearts."

(This last statement shows that Our Lady was indeed communicating with the children through the rays of light emanating from her, and not through verbal communication alone.)

Francisco, referring to the onlookers, then said, "These people are so happy just because you told them that Our Lady wants the rosary said, and that you are to learn to read! How would they feel if they only knew what she showed to us in God, in her Immaculate Heart, in that great light! But this is a secret. It must not be spoken about. It is better that no one should know it." Francisco had just celebrated his 9th birthday two days earlier.

Many of the residents of Aljustrel still believed that Lucia and her cousins had simply imagined all these encounters but some accused them of outright lying and so Maria Rosa and her brother Ti, the father of Jacinta and Francisco, took the three children to the local parish priest, Father Ferreira. After questioning the children, the priest came to the conclusion that it made no sense for Our Lady to make an appearance in order to ask the people to pray the rosary each day as most people did this anyway. He also noted that the children were unwilling to divulge all the information that they claimed they had been given. He observed that in instances where divine revelations had been made in the past, that the person receiving them would have to divulge everything. He then suggested that if they had indeed experienced something supernatural then it could have been of satanic origin!

These comments by their local priest were devastating for Lucia and her cousins and caused them a great deal of anguish. Lucia's response was to seek solitude and after this she would wander off to be alone, even avoiding Jacinta and Francisco. As she considered the comments made by the priest, she resolved not to go back to the Cova on the 13th of July. Francisco pleaded with her on a few occasions to change her mind and even stayed awake the whole night praying to Our Lady for Lucia to have a change of heart. It must have worked, because on that morning she felt an irresistible pull to go back to the Cova again.

3rd apparition: 13th July

By now, word of the apparitions had spread and so on Friday 13th July there were about four thousand people lining the streets waiting to accompany the children. When they reached the Cova da Iria, the crowds began praying with many of them saying the rosary out loud together. As Lucia, Francisco and Jacinta approached the sapling oak, there were flashes of bright light and then Our Lady once again appeared above the tree.

Lucia boldly asked, "What do you want of me?"

Our Lady replied, "I want you to come here on the 13th of next month, to continue to pray the rosary every day, in honour of Our Lady of the Rosary, in order to obtain peace for the world and the end of the war, because only she can help you."

Lucia, clearly upset by the locals and her parish priest disbelieving her, then asked, "I would like to ask you to tell us who you are, and to work a miracle so that everybody will believe that you are appearing to us."

Our Lady replied, "Continue to come here every month. **In October I will tell you who I am and what I want, and I will perform a miracle for all to see and believe**."

(The young Bernadette at Lourdes was treated in a very similar way to Lucia, and the disbelief of the villagers is reminiscent of the crowds that refused to believe in the divinity of Jesus unless he constantly worked miracles in front of their eyes. Jesus himself stated that his miracles should be seen as evidence that he was God's son.

"Why then do you accuse me of blasphemy because I said, 'I am God's son'? Do not believe me unless I do what my Father does. But if I do it, even though you do not believe me, believe the evidence of the miracles that you may know and understand that the Father is in me, and I in the Father." **John 10:36**)

Lucia also asked for the healing of several villagers and Our Lady replied by saying that the sick must pray the rosary in order to obtain the grace of healing. She added, **"Sacrifice yourself for sinners, and say many times, especially when you make some sacrifice: 'O Jesus, it is for love of You, for the conversion of sinners, and in reparation for sins committed against the Immaculate Heart of Mary.'"**

After saying this, she opened her hands to reveal the intense light in which the children were once again immersed, but on this occasion they were then given a terrifying vision of Hell.

(This vision of Hell would remain a secret until Lucia finally wrote it down on 31st August 1941, and it was after this that the Vatican subsequently published 'The Message and Secret of Fatima' on **13th May 1942**.)

"The rays of light seemed to penetrate the earth, and we saw, as it were a sea of fire. Plunged in this fire were demons and souls in human form, like transparent burning embers, all blackened or burnished bronze, floating about in the conflagration, now raised into the air by the flames that issued from within themselves together with great clouds of smoke, now falling back on every side like sparks in huge fires, without weight or equilibrium, amid shrieks and groans of pain and despair, which horrified us and made us tremble with fear. The demons could be distinguished by their terrifying and repellent likeness to frightful and unknown animals, black and transparent like burning coals. Terrified and as if to plead for succour, we looked up at Our Lady, who said to us, so kindly and so sadly:

"You have seen hell where the souls of poor sinners go. To save them, God wishes to establish in the world devotion to my Immaculate Heart. If what I say to you is done, many souls will be saved and there will be peace. The war is going to end; but if people do not cease offending God, a worse one will break out during the pontificate of Pius XI. When you see a **night illumined by an unknown light**, know that this is the great sign given you by God that He is about to punish the world for its crimes, by means of war, famine and persecutions of the Church and of the Holy Father. To prevent this, I shall come to ask for the **consecration of Russia to my Immaculate Heart**, and the **Communion of Reparation on the First Saturdays**. If my requests are heeded, Russia will be converted, and there will be peace; if not, she will spread her errors throughout the world, causing wars and persecutions of the Church. The good will be martyred, the Holy Father will have much to suffer, various nations will be annihilated. In the end, my Immaculate Heart will triumph. The Holy Father will consecrate Russia to me, and she will be converted, and a period of peace will be granted to the world. In Portugal, the dogma of the faith will always be preserved ..."

After saying this, Lucia, Francisco and Jacinta were given another vision, which later came to be known as the **Third Secret of Fatima**.

After this vision had been revealed to the children, Our Lady said, "Do not tell this to anybody. Francisco, yes, you may tell him."

She also said: **"When you pray the rosary, say, after each mystery: 'O my Jesus, forgive us, save us from the fires of hell. Lead all souls to heaven, especially those who are most in need."**

Finally Lucia asked, "Is there anything more that you want of me?" Our Lady replied, "No, I do not want any more of you today."

Then, as after the other appearances, Our Lady rose in an easterly direction and soon disappeared from their view. Lucia later wrote what Francisco had said of the rays of light that they had been immersed in:

"We were on fire with that light which is God, and yet we were not burnt! What is God? We could never put it into words. Yes, that is something indeed which we could never express! But what a pity it is that He is so sad! If only I could console him!"

(The 'fire' that the children saw, which in some ways resembles the appearance of physical fire, but which does not combust material immersed in it, is reminiscent of what Moses witnessed with the burning bush. Exodus 3:2: 'There the angel of the Lord appeared to him in flames of fire from within a bush. Moses saw that though the bush was on fire, it did not burn up.')

The vision of Hell left a lasting impression on the children, especially Jacinta, who was filled with horror at what she'd seen. After seeing this vision, any penance or sacrifice that she made, even if it caused her suffering, was as nothing if it could only help prevent some souls from going to Hell.

Lucia recalled in her third memoir that Jacinta would often sit on the ground and say, "Oh Hell! Hell! How sorry I am for the souls who go to Hell! And the people down there, burning alive, like wood in the fire!" She would then kneel down for long periods of time reciting the prayer that Our Lady had given the children: **"O my Jesus! Forgive us, save us from the fire of Hell. Lead all souls to Heaven, especially those who are most in need."**

After this vision, Jacinta regularly intervened if she heard children or even adults within earshot speaking crudely or saying anything unkind and she would tell them plainly that they were offending God. It was as though she put aside any concern for her own embarrassment or popularity so as to ensure that they steered away from sin.

Lucia also recalls her saying, "Francisco! Francisco! Are you praying with me? We must pray very much, to save souls from Hell! So many go there! So many!"

And on another occasion she asked Lucia, "Why doesn't Our Lady show Hell to sinners? If they saw it, they would not sin, so as to avoid going there! You must tell Our Lady to show Hell to all the people. You'll see how they will be converted."

Sometimes Jacinta would pick wild flowers and sing a hymn she had made up herself, "Sweet Heart of Mary, be my salvation! Immaculate Heart of Mary, convert sinners, save souls from Hell!"

So the first secret revealed to the children was the vision of Hell, and the second secret was a request for the consecration of Russia to the Immaculate Heart of Mary and the establishment of a devotion to her through the Communion of Reparation on the First Five Saturdays.

However on 13th July 1917, Our Lady said that the children should keep these revelations a secret i.e. a secret at that time. She gave no specifics about the Communion of Reparation devotion to her, and she also said that she would return later to ask for the Consecration of Russia to Her Immaculate Heart. The children therefore did as they'd been instructed and kept quiet about all these revelations.

(It was only on **10th December 1925** that Our Lady appeared to Lucia with the child Jesus in her room at the Dorothean convent near Pontevedra in Spain, and it was then that she gave specific details of the **First Five Saturday's devotion**.

On **15th February 1926**, the child Jesus again appeared to her, this time in the convent gardens, and again asked for this devotion to Our Lady, and Lucia then revealed this request to her confessor and also to the Mother Superior of the convent.

Our Lady then appeared to Lucia on **13th June 1929** when she was at the Dorothean Novitiate near Tuy, to ask for the **consecration of Russia to Her Immaculate Heart**, and Lucia then wrote an account of this revelation for her confessor, Father Goncalves. More detail on these three appearances to Lucia are given later in the book.

The secret of the vision of Hell was only revealed in Lucia's third memoir which she finished writing on **31st August 1941** while she was at Tuy. The third secret caused enormous controversy for decades, with the faithful speculating on why the Church had not released Lucia's account of the prophetic vision at all. Later, after its eventual release, there was controversy over whether or not the entire transcript had been made public and on what elements of the vision may have been withheld. It's incredible that the Vatican only made the contents of the third secret known on **26th June 2000**, about 83 years after the vision had first been given to Lucia, and this is also covered later.)

Even after the 13th July apparition, Maria Rosa was still convinced that Lucia was lying and so she again dragged her off to the parish priest to get her to admit to this. However after being questioned by the priest in great detail about what she'd seen, Lucia defiantly refused to recant.

The mayor of the town of Ourem, which had jurisdiction over Fatima, was a young man named Artur de Oliveira Santos, and he sent a message to the Marto and Dos Santos homes to say that he wanted to interview all three of the children in Ourem, which was nine miles away. Francisco and Jacinta's father wouldn't allow them to go for questioning as he felt that they were too young, but Lucia's parents were quite happy for her to go there and answer the mayor's questions.

So early the next day, Lucia accompanied by her father and her uncle, set off for Ourem, with Lucia riding on a donkey, which she fell off three times along the way. At the administration office, attempts were made to force Lucia to reveal what she'd seen and heard, and for her to promise never to return to the Cova da Iria again. Artur de Oliveira Santos made all manner of threats against Lucia, but she refused to talk and in the end she was released and allowed to go home.

(This is similar to what happened to Bernadette at Lourdes, where after the 6th apparition on 21st February 1858, she was taken to the Police Commissioner's house to be interrogated. However an angry crowd gathered outside his home and Bernadette was released. She was again interrogated after the 9th apparition by the town's Imperial Prosecutor and later by a magistrate after the 11th apparition. As with Lucia, the young Bernadette had to face her local priests who were disbelieving of her accounts. It was only after the 16th apparition on 25th March 1858, when Bernadette repeated to Father Peyramale the words of Our Lady, **"I am the Immaculate Conception"** that he finally believed her. This doctrine of the Church had only been recognised four years earlier and it would have been impossible for Bernadette to have made this up. Fittingly the 25th of March is the Feast of the Annunciation.)

The large crowds that had descended on the Cova meant that Lucia's family could no longer grow vegetables as the whole area had been churned up by the feet of thousands of visitors. Lucia's mother was now distraught but she still couldn't get her daughter to admit to lying despite her verbal threats and occasional beatings with a broom handle.

Lucia was later questioned in minute detail by the Reverend Dr Formigao, but despite the thoroughness of his examination she would not reveal the secrets nor did she contradict herself under questioning. Lucia actually became very fond of him and he then came on a regular basis to interview her on the events at the Cova da Iria.

On Monday 13th August 1917, great crowds had gathered in the village in the hope that they might see Our Lady. However the children were unable to walk to the Cova that day due to another intervention by Artur de Oliviera Santos, and what he did to the children that day would be unthinkable in our modern world.

He sent a message to Lucia's home instructing her to go immediately to her aunt's house, and so Antonio walked with his daughter the short distance over to the Marto's home, which was difficult in itself due to the massive crowds that had now gathered there.

Many villagers wanted to ask the children what Our Lady had said, and other people were pleading for the children to petition her to cure their relatives of various illnesses. But when Antonio and Lucia arrived at the house, they found that Artur was already there and he quickly set about interrogating the children in order to extricate the secrets that they'd been given, but he was again unsuccessful.

He then took the children to the house of the Parish priest, Father Ferreira, but after a short while he put them in his horse-drawn carriage and drove them off to Ourem without their parent's knowledge or consent.

When word reached the crowds that the children had been taken to Ourem instead of being allowed to go to the Cova, there was a near riot. In Ourem, the children were questioned yet again about what had happened at the Cova da Iria but they all still refused to talk.

Later that day, and after various threats were made against them, they were thrown into a communal cell which was the public jail of the town. They were told that they had to wait there while a cauldron of oil was boiled and that if they did not confide their secrets then they would be executed in it, one at a time.

It beggars belief that children could be treated in this way, and poor Jacinta, who was born on 11th March 1910, was only seven years old at the time. Even the other prisoners in the cell tried to get the children to talk, either to save them from harm or perhaps in an attempt to get themselves released from prison. Jacinta, believing that she was about to die, took a religious medal from her pocket and asked one of the prisoners to hang it on a nail in the wall for her.

She knelt down to pray the rosary with Lucia and Francisco, and incredibly the other prisoners knelt down to pray with them. But as he sat in the cell, Francisco became increasingly distressed that they would be unable to meet Our Lady at the Cova as she had asked them to do.

He later said, "Our Lady must have been very sad because we didn't go to the Cova da Iria, and she won't appear to us again. I would so love to see her!"

After a few hours, they were removed from the cell and locked in another room believing that their execution was now imminent. Still they refused to talk and so Jacinta was taken out first and led away, and some time later they returned to take Francisco away too, leaving poor Lucia all alone in the dark room. The door was then unlocked for a third time, and then Lucia was led away too, but to her immense relief it was not to be executed in boiling oil but to another room where her cousins were waiting for her, still alive and well.

Artur kept them in Ourem for another night but when he finally realised that they weren't going to talk, he took them back to Fatima in his carriage and left them outside the presbytery of the church, not even bothering to take the traumatised children home to their families.

4th apparition: 19th August

On the Sunday following their release from custody in Ourem, Lucia, Francisco, and his older brother Joao were tending their sheep at Valinhos near Aljustrel, with Joao Marto being one of the children who had been with Lucia when the angel appeared to her for the second time in 1915.

Prior to seeing anything unusual at all, the three children could feel something supernatural approaching them. Lucia wanted Jacinta to be present and so she asked Joao to run back to the house and fetch her. At about 4pm, there was a brilliant flash of light in the sky as had preceded all the other apparitions, and immediately after this, the children saw Our Lady above the Holm Oak sapling once again.

Lucia then asked her customary question, "What do you want of me?"

Our Lady replied, "I want you to continue going to the Cova da Iria on the 13th and to continue praying the rosary every day. **In the last month, I will perform a miracle so that all may believe.**"

Lucia asked, "What do you want done with the money the people leave in the Cova da Iria?"

She answered, "Have two litters made. One is to be carried by you and Jacinta and two other girls dressed in white; the other one is to be carried by Francisco and three other boys. The money from the litters is for the festa of Our Lady of the Rosary, and what is left over will help towards the construction of a chapel that is to be built here."

Lucia then said, "I would like to ask you to cure some sick persons."

To this, Our Lady replied, "Yes, I will cure some of them during the year."

Lucia said that Our Lady looked very sad as she then said, **"Pray, pray very much, and make sacrifices for sinners; for many souls go to hell, because there are none to sacrifice themselves and to pray for them."**

Unlike at her other appearances, Our Lady did not immerse the children in the light from her hands on this occasion but simply rose up and disappeared from their view in an easterly direction. After this visit, the children thought up all manner of ways to offer little sacrifices to God including wearing a rope tied tightly around their waists which caused them a lot of discomfort. They would often go without food or drink and they would give their lunches away to the poor children they encountered along the path that led to the fields.

It's important to note that only the children could see Our Lady at these apparitions, but the crowds couldn't see her at all, although they sometimes saw the phenomena associated with her presence. Francisco was overjoyed that Our Lady had returned again as he'd been having doubts since his imprisonment in Ourem that she would do so.

Many of the visitors to the Cova da Iria came on mules, and the land had been so trodden underfoot that it was now useless for growing their vegetables or to provide pasture for their sheep. Maria Rosa reluctantly had to sell the flock, with the exception of three sheep as they were so in need of money. Lucia was constantly being sought out by a never-ending stream of people asking to speak to her about what she'd seen, what Our Lady had said to her, and to give her more petitions. In addition to this, she was continually being called to give an account of herself to priests from other dioceses as well as to the local parish priest. Unfortunately many of the villagers still thought that the children were lying and on some occasions Lucia was kicked or slapped across the face in addition to the verbal abuse that she was being given.

5th apparition: 13th September

A massive crowd of about thirty thousand started making their way towards the Cova da Iria in anticipation of another apparition, with huge numbers of people pressing against the children, some falling to their knees begging them to petition Our Lady for a miraculous cure or for some other request. As they walked one woman in the crowd even reached out and grabbed Lucia's hair cutting off her plaits, but Lucia was unperturbed by all of this commotion. People frantically climbed the trees along the route, and others stood on top of the walls all the way along the road from Aljustrel to Fatima, and they shouted down to the children as they walked by. Lucia said that the chaotic scene reminded her of the Gospel accounts in which Jesus was mobbed by thousands of people as he walked from town to town.

When they reached the Holm Oak at the Cova da Iria, the majority of the crowd knelt down to pray the rosary with many calling aloud for the healing of their family members who were ill. The children also began to pray the rosary and shortly after this there was a brilliant flash of light and soon afterwards our Lady was there with them, standing above the tree.

She said, "Continue to pray the rosary in order to obtain the end of the war. In October Our Lord will come, as well as Our Lady of Dolours and Our Lady of Carmel. Saint Joseph will appear with the Child Jesus to bless the world. God is pleased with your sacrifices. He does not want you to sleep with the rope on, but only to wear it during the day time."

Lucia said, "I was told to ask you many things, the cure of some sick people, of a deaf mute ..."

She replied, "Yes, I will cure some, but not others. **In October I will perform a miracle so that all may believe.**"

Again there were no rays emanating from Our Lady's hands on this appearance but Francisco was overjoyed when Lucia told him that Jesus would appear with Our Lady at her next visit.

Although the crowd couldn't see the Virgin Mary, two other supernatural events were observed by thousands of people that day. Shortly before the appearance of Our Lady, the sky darkened at around midday and a luminous globe or 'ball of fire' as some described it, was seen moving through the sky. Most said that the bright object was oval and not perfectly round and moving far too fast to have possibly been the sun, and Padre Joao Quaresma who witnessed the phenomenon described it as follows:

"To my great astonishment I saw, clearly and distinctly, a luminous globe coming from the east and moving to the west, gliding slowly and majestically through space. With my hand I motioned to Monsignor Gois who was standing next to me, and who had been making fun of me for coming. Looking up he too saw this unexpected vision. Then suddenly this globe, giving off an extraordinary light, disappeared from my sight, and Monsignor Gois, also, saw it no longer."

The second phenomenon occurred as Our Lady left, and her departure was accompanied by the falling to earth of white 'petals' surrounded by a supernatural light and these were described as looking like round, shining snowflakes. The phenomenon was also unusual in that the luminescent objects became smaller as they got closer to earth, instead of appearing bigger, before vanishing without a trace.

- Chapter 3 -

The Miracle of the Sun

Even by the beginning of October 1917, many people were unconvinced that the apparitions were real, and rumours began circulating that the authorities had planned to detonate a bomb close to the site of the apparitions to dissuade people from gathering there. However, the events that would unfold this day would shatter any illusion that the children had been lying and the reaction of those in the great crowd that had gathered would be just like that of the doubting Thomas, who on touching the risen Jesus standing in front of him could only utter the words, "My Lord and my God."

6th apparition: 13th October

Lucia, Jacinta and Francisco left home very early on the morning of Saturday 13th October, as they thought it likely that they'd be delayed by all the people along the way. Heavy rain was falling, and already there were massive crowds lining the roads. Lucia's parents were concerned for her safety, so they decided to go with her to the Cova for the first time, and her father walked the route holding Lucia's hand.

It's thought that about 70,000 people arrived on the hillside in great anticipation of seeing a miracle on this day, although some estimates put the number as high as 100,000. Either way, it was a massive crowd that had gathered in the torrential rain, and they soon trampled the Cova into a field of mud. Lucia asked the crowds to close their umbrellas and to pray the rosary, and despite the awful conditions the crowds went down on their knees in the mud to pray.

Then a distinctive blue-coloured column of smoke was seen rising to a height of about two to three metres above the heads of the children. This smoke column, which dissipated after a minute or so, had been witnessed on the previous five visits by Our Lady as well. By now the oak tree at the site of the apparitions had been stripped of its foliage by people wanting to take a leaf or two home with them as a souvenir. The townsfolk had however built a wooden arch at the site and so Lucia, Jacinta and Francisco went there instead. Lucia then asked the crowds to start reciting the rosary once again, which they did.

After seeing the brilliant flash of light which preceded all the apparitions, Our Lady appeared in their midst above the ground, with Lucia then making her innocent declaration of faith, saying, "What do you want of me?"

Our Lady answered, "I want to tell you that a chapel is to be built here in my honour. **I am the Lady of the Rosary**. Continue always to pray the rosary every day. The war is going to end, and the soldiers will soon return to their homes."

Lucia then said, "I have many things to ask you: the cure of some sick persons, the conversion of sinners, and other things…"

Our Lady replied, "Some yes, but not others. They must amend their lives and ask forgiveness for their sins."

She went on, **"Do not offend the Lord our God any more, because He is already so much offended."**

Lucia wrote that Our Lady looked deeply saddened when she said these words.

After saying this, Our Lady then opened her hands and projected her own light onto the sun as she ascended into the sky, and it was at this moment that Lucia said that she immediately felt an interior impulse to call out, "Look at the sun!"

She wrote: "After Our Lady had disappeared into the immense distance of the firmament, we beheld St Joseph with the child Jesus and Our Lady robed in white with a blue mantle, beside the sun. St Joseph and the Child Jesus appeared to bless the world, for they traced the Sign of the Cross with their hands.

"When, a little later, this Apparition disappeared, I saw Our Lord and Our Lady; it seemed to me that it was Our Lady of Dolours. Our Lord appeared to bless the world in the same manner as St Joseph had done. This apparition also vanished, and I saw Our Lady once more, this time resembling Our Lady of Carmel."

There are many eyewitness accounts of the breathtaking solar phenomenon that tens of thousands of people witnessed that day. Terrified onlookers describe having seen the sun spin wildly in the sky, and at one point fall towards the Earth, before returning to its normal size and position. The event was witnessed not just by the massive crowd at the Cova but by people up to eighteen kilometres away. Despite this, no observatories recorded anything unusual that day, further indicating that it was a relatively localised miraculous event.

There had been a great downpour of rain just prior to the Miracle of the Sun and so the massive crowd were soaking wet and the fields were completely sodden at the time. However immediately after the inexplicable movements of the sun, observers reported that the ground and their clothing had become completely dry.

De Marchi, a scientist who studied the events at Fatima, wrote: "Engineers that have studied the case reckoned that an incredible amount of energy would have been necessary to dry up those pools of water that had formed on the field in a few minutes, as it was reported by witnesses."

Below is an account of the events that was written by Doctor Almeida Garrett, who was the professor of the Faculty of Science at Coimbra University.

"It must have been 1:30 pm when there arose, at the exact spot where the children were, a column of smoke, thin, fine and bluish, which extended up to perhaps two meters above their heads, and evaporated at that height. This phenomenon, perfectly visible to the naked eye, lasted for a few seconds. Not having noted how long it had lasted, I cannot say whether it was more or less than a minute. The smoke dissipated abruptly, and after some time, it came back to occur a second time, then a third time.

"I was looking at the spot of the apparitions in a serene, if cold, expectation of something happening and with diminishing curiosity because a long time had passed without anything to excite my attention. The sun, a few moments before, had broken through the thick layer of clouds which hid it and now shone clearly and intensely.

"Suddenly I heard the uproar of thousands of voices, and I saw the whole multitude spread out in that vast space at my feet, turn their backs to that spot where, until then, all their expectations had been focused, and look at the sun on the other side. I turned around, too, toward the point commanding their gaze and I could see the sun, like a very clear disc, with its sharp edge, which gleamed without hurting the sight.

"The most astonishing thing was to be able to stare at the solar disc for a long time, brilliant with light and heat, without hurting the eyes or damaging the retina. During this time, the sun's disc did not remain immobile, it had a giddy motion, but not like the twinkling of a star in all its brilliance, for it spun round upon itself in a mad whirl.

"During the solar phenomenon, which I have just described, there were also changes of colour in the atmosphere. Looking at the sun, I noticed that everything was becoming darkened. I looked first at the nearest objects and then extended my glance further afield as far as the horizon. I saw everything had assumed an amethyst colour. Objects around me, the sky and the atmosphere, were of the same colour. Everything both near and far had changed, taking on the colour of old yellow damask. People looked as if they were suffering from jaundice and I recall a sensation of amusement at seeing them look so ugly and unattractive. My own hand was the same colour.

"Then, suddenly, one heard a clamor, a cry of anguish breaking from all the people. The sun, whirling wildly, seemed all at once to loosen itself from the firmament and, blood red, advance threateningly upon the earth as if to crush us with its huge and fiery weight. The sensation during those moments was truly terrible.

"All the phenomena which I have described were observed by me in a calm and serene state of mind without any emotional disturbance. It is for others to interpret and explain them. Finally, I must declare that never, before or after October 13 (1917), have I observed similar atmospheric or solar phenomena."

Doctor Domingos Pinto Coelho wrote an article on this spectacular event for the Ordem newspaper:

"The sun, at one moment surrounded with scarlet flame, at another aureoled in yellow and deep purple, seemed to be in an exceedingly swift and whirling movement, at times appearing to be loosened from the sky and to be approaching the earth, strongly radiating heat."

The Reverend Joaquin Laurenco also described what he saw that day, when he was a boy living in Alburitel, eighteen kilometres from Fatima:

"I feel incapable of describing what I saw. I looked fixedly at the sun, which seemed pale and did not hurt my eyes. Looking like a ball of snow, revolving on itself, it suddenly seemed to come down in a zigzag, menacing the earth. Terrified, I ran and hid myself among the people, who were weeping and expecting the end of the world at any moment."

Alfredo de Silva Santos was also present that day, and he wrote:

"When Lucia called out, 'Look at the sun!' the whole multitude echoed, 'Look at the sun!' It was a day of incessant drizzle, but a few moments before the miracle it left off raining. I can hardly find words to describe what followed. The sun began to move, and at a certain moment appeared to be detached from the sky and about to hurtle on us like a wheel of flame. My wife – we had been married only a short time – fainted. I fell on my knees oblivious of everything, and when I got up I don't know what I said. I think I began to cry out like the others."

Avelino de Almeida wrote an article about it for the Seculo newspaper:

"The sun trembled, made sudden incredible movements outside all cosmic laws – the sun 'danced' according to the typical expression of the people. They began to ask each other what they had seen. The great majority admitted to having seen the trembling and the dancing of the sun; others affirmed that they saw the face of the Blessed Virgin; others, again, saw that the sun whirled on itself like a giant catherine wheel and that it lowered itself to the earth as if to burn it in its rays. Some said they saw it change colours successively."

An article on the phenomenon was also printed in the O Dia newspaper on 17th October 1917:

"At one o' clock in the afternoon, midday by the sun, the rain stopped. The sky, pearly grey in colour, illuminated the vast arid landscape with a strange light. The sun had a transparent gauzy veil so that the eyes could easily be fixed upon it. The grey mother-of-pearl tone turned into a sheet of silver which broke up as the clouds were torn apart, and the silver sun, enveloped in the same gauzy grey light, was seen to whirl and turn in the circle of broken clouds.

"A cry went up from every mouth and people fell on their knees on the muddy ground. The light turned a beautiful blue as if it had come through the stained-glass windows of a cathedral and spread itself over the people who knelt with outstretched hands. The blue faded slowly, and then the light seemed to pass through yellow glass. Yellow stains fell against white handkerchiefs, against the dark skirts of the women.

They were repeated on the trees, on the stones and on the serra. People wept and prayed with uncovered heads in the presence of the miracle they had awaited. The seconds seemed like hours, so vivid were they."

Another person at the Cova da Iria that day was Dona Maria do Carmo da Cruz Menezes, who said:

"Suddenly the rain stopped and the sun broke through, casting its rays on the earth. It seemed to be falling on that vast crowd of people and it spun like a fire-wheel, taking on all the colours of the rainbow. We ourselves took on those colours, with our clothes and even the earth itself. One heard cries and saw many people in tears. Deeply impressed, I said to myself: 'My God, how great is your power!'"

Bishop da Silva, who was the Bishop of Leiria-Fatima at the time, wrote the following about the solar phenomenon:

"The children had foretold the day and the hour at which the solar phenomenon would occur. The news spread rapidly throughout Portugal, and in spite of bad weather, thousands and thousands of people congregated at the spot. At the hour of the last Apparition, they witnessed all the manifestations of the sun which paid homage to the Queen of Heaven and earth, more brilliant than the heavenly body itself at its zenith of light.

"This phenomenon, which was not registered in any astronomical observatory, and could not, therefore, have been of natural origin, was witnessed by people of every category and class, by believers as well as unbelievers, journalists of the principal daily papers and even by people kilometres away, a fact which destroys any theory of collective hallucination."

Many miracles have been associated with Fatima, but one of the earliest was the healing of Higino Faria, who had suffered terribly for many years from a type of paralysis. He was instantaneously healed on 13th October 1917, the very day of the Miracle of the Sun, with his incredulous doctors all affirming to his cure and unable to offer a scientific explanation for it.

Just three weeks after the Miracle of the Sun, the Russian Civil War began on 7th November 1917, in which Lenin's Bolshevics or Red Army under Leon Trotsky fought against their own countrymen, the White Russians. During this mayhem, the Russian Royal Family was kept under house arrest at Tobolsk in Siberia, until Lenin ordered their execution on 16th July 1918.

News of the Miracle of the Sun spread like wildfire, and resulted in massive numbers of people visiting the site of the apparitions. Some villagers erected wooden poles to form an arch from which they suspended lanterns and they ensured that these were always lit, night and day. But the local Government disapproved of what was happening and ordered that the arch be dismantled and that the Holm Oak be removed. Whether the men carrying out these instructions did it deliberately or not, we will never know, but it was the wrong tree that they removed and Lucia was greatly relieved at this. On 6th August 1918, the Feast of the Transfiguration, the local villagers began to build a chapel on the site of the apparitions, just as Our Lady had requested.

At the final apparition, Our Lady had said that the war would soon end, and the conflict did indeed end on 11th November 1918 when the Armistice was signed. But although World War I was over, hostilities in Europe continued as a consequence of the Russian Civil War. Poland invaded the Ukraine in 1920 and fought against the Red Army, until the Treaty of Riga ended hostilities between Soviet Russia, Soviet Ukraine and Poland on 18th March 1921. This brought ten million White Russians under Polish control, but ultimately the Bolshevics won the Russian Civil War and Russia then became a communist state.

The figure given for the total number of casualties in World War I varies greatly depending on the value that is attributed to war-related disease and famine, but 37 million is a figure that is often cited. Over 9 million combatants and 6.5 million civilians perished in the fighting, but many of the surviving soldiers suffered life-changing injuries.

As an example, there were 1.77 million German military fatalities in the war, but in addition to this, another 4.2 million men were injured in the conflict. The British Army suffered 1.65 million casualties, of which 240,000 required total or partial amputations.

As at Guadalupe in 1531, and Lourdes in 1858, Our Lady had appeared at Fatima to offer hope and to show mankind the way to God's love, and at all three of these great Marian apparitions, she had worked spectacular miracles to prove the reality of her presence on earth.

- Chapter 4 -

Two more saints in heaven

It's incredible that Lucia's own mother still had doubts about the apparitions even after the Miracle of the Sun, but sometime later she became seriously ill and appeared to be very close to death. Lucia and her siblings gathered around her bed, and one by one they said their last goodbyes to her. In desperation, as Lucia left the bedroom her two older sisters came to her saying, "Lucia! If it is true that you saw Our Lady, go right now to the Cova da Iria and ask her to cure our mother. Promise her whatever you wish and we'll do it, and then we'll believe."

Lucia left immediately and went to the Cova saying the rosary as she went, and at the site of the apparitions she cried and prayed that Our Lady would heal her dying mother. She said that if her mother was cured, then she would visit the site every day for nine consecutive days with her sisters. They would walk on their knees from the road to the Holm Oak, and pray the rosary there together. She promised that on the ninth day, they would find nine poor children to take with them to the Holm oak to pray and that they would give them a meal afterwards. Lucia's prayers were answered, and Maria Rosa miraculously came back from the brink of death and went on to make a full recovery.

From January 1918 until December 1920, there was an influenza pandemic which is estimated to have killed at least 50 million people worldwide or 3% of the Earth's population at that time, but some estimates are as high as 100 million deaths. As an example of the scale of the outbreak, 17 million people died in India, representing 5% of the entire population, and on the island of Fiji, 14% of the population died in just two weeks.

In 1918, the major world powers of Britain, Germany, France and the USA censored their press on what they could print on the pandemic in order to preserve morale at home. However in Spain, which was neutral, the press reported freely and this gave the impression that the outbreak was far worse there than anywhere else and so it was referred to as 'Spanish Flu.'

Research by virologists at St Bartholomew's hospital and the Royal London hospital indicated that the outbreak centered on the town of

Etaples, near Boulogne in France. It's thought that the precursor virus of this lethal strain was the H1N1 (Avian Flu) virus found in birds. Etaples was a staging post for troop deployment at the end of World War I, and in Etaples there were massive numbers of chickens in close proximity to pigs in order to supply food for the troops.

The H1N1 virus is thought to have mutated in the pigs, and it was then able to cross the species barrier and pass on to man as a sub-type of the Avian Flu virus. It's thought that Spanish Flu killed even more people than the Black Death, and the majority of the deaths resulted from a secondary bacterial (not viral) pneumonia that developed under the suppressed immune system conditions. The mortality rate was at least 10%. Unfortunately, at this time in history, immunisations were not available to prevent the influenza infection, nor were there antibiotics to control the secondary bacterial infections, such as bacterial pneumonia.

(Various researchers had noticed that Penicillium fungal moulds had an inhibitory effect on the development of bacteria, including Alexander Fleming, a Scottish biologist. In 1928 he noticed that some of his Staphylococcus culture trays had been contaminated by a blue-green mould. There was a ring around the fungal mould which was preventing the Staphylococcus bacteria from advancing beyond it. He grew a pure culture of the mould, which he identified as Penicillium notatum, and over the next twelve years he grew and distributed the mould. However it was not until 1941 that large scale production of stable Penicillin was possible, in order to treat bacterial infections.)

After the apparition of 13th October 1917, Francisco had said to Lucia: "I loved seeing Our Lord, but I loved still more seeing Him in that light where we were with Him as well. It's not long now, and Our Lord will take me up close to Him, and then I can look at Him forever."

He would increasingly wander off on his own to pray, and to offer small sacrifices to Jesus. Lucia and Jacinta would usually find him at one of his favourite haunts, which was by the side of the well. Jacinta's focus was on the conversion of sinners and trying to save people from going to Hell, but Francisco was always concerned with consoling Jesus and Our Lady through his prayers and sacrifices. Francisco was also empathetic to the sufferings of the sick people that he met, and he often prayed for them as well.

When they were on their way to school in Fatima, Francisco sometimes urged Lucia to go on ahead of him, saying that he would prefer to stay with the 'hidden Jesus' in the church all day. He said there was no point in him learning how to read as he would be going to Heaven very soon anyway. Lucia would find him still there on her way home from school several hours later.

Francisco fell ill with the Spanish flu in late October 1918, and he spent over five months suffering from its effects. On some days, when he could hardly walk, he still somehow made it to the church to be with the 'hidden Jesus' and he would wait there until Lucia returned on her way back from school. But when he was too ill to even get out of bed, Lucia would go over to visit him, and sometimes she would ask if he was suffering a great deal.

He would reply, "Quite a lot, but never mind! I am suffering to console Our Lord, and afterwards, within a short time, I am going to Heaven!"

While sick in bed, he was often visited by people with petitions. One of these was a woman from Alqueidao, who asked him to pray for her friend who was gravely ill, and also for the conversion of another person that she knew. Although very ill himself, Francisco agreed to pray for them both.

Francisco died on 4th April 1919, aged just ten, and both of his parents noticed that he had died with a smile on his face. Two days earlier, he had made his first confession, and he then made his first communion the following day, the day before he died. He was overjoyed at receiving communion, and Jacinta and Lucia spent most of that day with him by his bedside.

Lucia said her final goodbye to Francisco that night, and she said to him, "Goodbye, Francisco! If you go to Heaven tonight, don't forget me when you get there, do you hear me?"

"No, I won't forget. Be sure of that," he replied. They were both crying and holding each other's hands as she said to him, "Goodbye then, Francisco! Till we meet in Heaven, goodbye!"

Francisco died the following day, and he was originally buried in the cemetery at Fatima. Shortly after his burial, the lady from Alqueidao came to Lucia and Jacinta asking them to take her to his grave so that she could give thanks for her petitions which had both been answered.

Unfortunately, Lucia's father later became ill himself, and Antonio died of double pneumonia on the 31st of July 1919. The man who had always stood by Lucia, and who had defended her when all the others were verbally abusing her, and the man who had bravely held Lucia's hand as they walked through a crowd of 70,000 before the Miracle of the Sun, was now gone.

Lucia was devastated by this loss, and she said this about her father: "He was the only one who never failed to show himself to be my friend, and the only one who defended me when disputes arose at home on account of me."

Jacinta had also contracted Spanish Flu about a month before Francisco, and she suffered from bronchial pneumonia and abscesses on the membrane (pleura) covering the lungs. Lucia recalled in her third memoir, which was written in Tuy in 1941, the extraordinary faith that the eight-year-old Jacinta had. Shortly before Jacinta was admitted to hospital she said to Lucia:

"It will not be long now before I go to Heaven. You will remain here to make known that God wishes to establish in the world devotion to the Immaculate Heart of Mary.

"When you are to say this, don't go and hide. Tell everybody that God grants us graces through the Immaculate Heart of Mary; that people are to ask her for them; and that the Heart of Jesus wants the Immaculate Heart of Mary to be venerated at His side. Tell them also to pray to the Immaculate Heart of Mary for peace, since God has entrusted it to her.

"If I could only put into the hearts of all, the fire that is burning within my own heart, and that makes me love the Hearts of Jesus and Mary so very much!"

She spent two months in St Augustine's hospital at Ourem without her family, although her mother and Lucia were sometimes able to visit her there. By the end of August 1918, her condition had deteriorated and she now had tuberculosis and pleurisy. The treatment wasn't working, and the poor family could no longer afford to pay the costs, and so she was then taken back to Aljustrel. By now she looked like a living skeleton, as bacteria had eaten away at her body tissues, but the brave eight-year-old said to Lucia that she was offering her sufferings for the conversion of sinners.

She would also kiss the crucifix and say, "O my Jesus! I love You, and I want to suffer very much for love of You. O Jesus! Now you can convert many sinners, because this is really a big sacrifice!"

Jacinta said that Our Lady had appeared to her during her suffering to give her comfort on a number of occasions, and she explained to Lucia what Our Lady had said to her on one of these visits:

"I am going to Lisbon to another hospital; I will not see you again, nor my parents either, and after suffering a great deal, I shall die alone. But she said I must not be afraid, since she herself is coming to take me to heaven."

In January 1920, Jacinta was placed in an orphanage in Lisbon, appropriately named Our Lady of the Miracles, and here she received Holy Communion every day, which was a great comfort to her. On the 2nd of February, Jacinta was taken to the Dona Estafania hospital, where she had an operation which involved making an insertion in her side to drain off the pus from two of her ribs. She had this operation without a general anaesthetic, and Doctor Leonardo, who conducted the procedure, was impressed with the bravery of the nine-year-old girl. However her condition worsened, and on 20th February 1920, Jacinta made her confession in the morning and passed away later that night.

Francisco was initially buried in a small cemetery in Fatima, but his remains were later moved to the sanctuary that had been built at the Cova da Iria, where the apparitions had taken place. Jacinta was buried in the grounds of Vila Nova de Ourem, but in 1935 her body was also interred in the sanctuary at Cova da Iria that held Francisco's remains. When her coffin was opened in 1935, her face was found to be incorrupt and undecayed.

On the 1st of May 1951, Jacinta's remains were moved to the Basilica of Our Lady of the Rosary of Fatima, and Francisco's remains were interred in the same basilica in March 1952. When Francisco's coffin was opened, he still had the rosary beads that he had been buried with, entwined around his fingers.

- Chapter 5 -

Subsequent apparitions

These were very testing times for Lucia, because since the appearance of Our Lady and the Miracle of the Sun on 13th October 1917, she had lost three of the people she cared most about in her life. Francisco, her father, and young Jacinta had all died within a period of only two years and four months of the miracle.

Lucia's mother decided to go to Lisbon for a time, and here she stayed with a lady named Dona Assuncao Avelar. Dona kindly offered to pay for Lucia's education at a boarding school, but before attending this school she briefly returned to the town of Aljustrel.

On the 25th of July 1920, Bishop Jose da Silva was installed as the new Bishop of Leiria and Jose would hold this office until 1957. He would go on to play a very important role in ensuring that the events at Fatima were communicated effectively through to the Vatican, and it was Bishop da Silva who would later declare that the apparitions at Fatima were indeed 'worthy of belief.'

On Thursday **16th June 1921**, Our Lady again appeared to Lucia who was now fourteen, with a private message which has never been made public. This was just before she left for the convent school in Vilar near Porto, which was a college run by the Dorothean Sisters, and here she used the name Maria dos Dores, or Mary of the Sorrows. After her schooling had finished, she then went to Pontevedra in Spain as a novice in the Dorothean Convent.

On the 29th of July 1921, Adolph Hitler became the leader of the National Socialist Party in Germany, the Nazi's. Back in Fatima, the little chapel or capelinha at the site of the apparitions was blown up with dynamite by enemies of the Catholic Church on 6th March 1922. However the villagers were undeterred by this and they soon rebuilt it, with the first mass being celebrated in the new church in January 1924.

Adolph Hitler attempted to seize power in Munich in a coup on the 8th and 9th of November 1923, but his 2000 strong mob were defeated, and Hitler was then arrested. He was sentenced to 5 years in prison but ultimately only served 9 months, before being released on 20th December 1924. During his imprisonment he dictated the text for his book, 'Mein Kampf' to his fellow prisoner, Rudolf Hess, and the book was later published on the 18th of July 1925.

It was in her room at the Dorothean convent on the **10th of December 1925**, that Our Lady again appeared to Lucia, and in this apparition she appeared with the child Jesus by her side, and Jesus was supported by a luminous cloud. Our Lady showed Lucia a heart which was encircled by thorns, which she held in her hand.

The child Jesus said, "Have compassion on the Heart of your Most Holy Mother, covered with thorns, with which ungrateful men pierce it at every moment, and there is no-one to make an act of reparation to remove them."

Our Lady then said:

"Look, my daughter, at my Heart, surrounded with thorns with which ungrateful men pierce me at every moment by their blasphemies and ingratitude. You can at least try to console me and say that I promise to assist at the hour of death, with the graces necessary for salvation, all those who, for five consecutive months, shall confess, receive Holy Communion, recite five decades of the rosary, and keep me company for fifteen minutes while meditating on the fifteen mysteries of the rosary, with the intention of making reparation to me."

Lucia wrote that Jesus again appeared to her two months later in the convent garden at Pontevedra on **15th February 1926**, which she described as follows:

"On the 15th (of February 1926), I was very busy with my chores, and I scarcely thought of it (the apparition of the preceding December 10th). I was about to empty the garbage can outside the garden. At the same place, several months previously, I had met a child whom I had asked if he knew the Hail Mary. He had replied, 'Yes', and I had asked him to say it for me, in order to hear him. But as he would not say it alone, I had recited it three times with him.

"At the end of the three Hail Mary's, I asked him to say it alone. As he remained silent and did not appear capable of saying it alone, I asked him if he knew the Church of Saint Mary. He answered, 'Yes.' I then told him to go there every day and to pray thus: 'Oh my Heavenly Mother, give me Your Child Jesus!'

"I taught him that prayer and departed. Then on February 15, while returning as usual (to empty a garbage can outside of the garden), I found there a child who appeared to me to be the same, and I then asked him: 'Have you asked Our Heavenly Mother for the Child Jesus?'

"The child turned to me and said: 'And have you revealed to the world what the Heavenly Mother has asked you?' And saying that, He transformed Himself into a resplendent child.

"Recognising then that it was Jesus, I said to Him: 'My Jesus! You know very well what my confessor said to me in the letter I read to you. He said that this vision had to be repeated; there had to be facts permitting us to believe it, and that the Mother Superior alone could not spread this devotion.'

"The child replied, 'It is true that the Mother Superior, alone, can do nothing, but with My grace, she can do anything. It is enough that your confessor gives you permission, and that your Superior announces this for it to be believed by the people, even if they do not know who it was revealed to.'

"I said, 'But my confessor said in his letter that this devotion already exists in the world, because many souls receive Thee every first Saturday of the month, in honor of Our Lady and the fifteen mysteries of the rosary.'

"The child replied, 'It is true, My daughter, that many souls begin, but few persevere to the very end, and those who persevere do it to receive the graces promised. The souls who make the Five First Saturdays with fervor and to make reparation to the Heart of your Heavenly Mother, please Me more than those who make fifteen, but are lukewarm and indifferent.'

"I said, 'My Jesus! Many souls find it difficult to confess on Saturday. Will You allow a confession within eight days to be valid?'

"The child replied, 'Yes. It can even be made later on, provided that the souls are in the state of grace when they receive Me on the first Saturday, and that they had the intention of making reparation to the Sacred Heart of Mary.'

"I said, 'My Jesus! And those who forget to form this intention?'

"The child replied, 'They can form it at the next confession, taking advantage of their first opportunity to go to confession.' After that the Child Jesus disappeared without saying anything more."

Lucia was soon moved to the Dorothean Novitiate in Tuy which is near Pontevedra in northwest Spain, where she finally made her vows on 3rd October 1928.

Then on **13th June 1929**, she was again visited by Our Lady, and this fulfilled the promise made twelve years earlier on 13th July 1917, when Our Lady had said that she would come back to ask for the consecration of Russia. This is how Lucia described the encounter:

"I had requested and obtained permission from my superiors and my confessor to make a holy hour from 11pm to midnight, from Thursday to Friday of each week. Finding myself alone one night, I knelt down near the Communion rail in the middle of the chapel, to recite the prayers of the Angel, lying prostrate. Feeling tired, I got up and continued to recite them with my arms in the form of a cross. The only light was that of the sanctuary lamp.

"Suddenly, the whole chapel lit up with a supernatural light, and on the altar appeared a cross of light which reached the ceiling. In a clearer light, on the upper part of the cross, could be seen the face of a man with His body to the waist, on His chest a dove, equally luminous; and nailed to the cross, the body of another man. A little below the waist (of Christ on the cross), suspended in the air, could be seen a Chalice and a large Host, onto which some drops of Blood were falling, which flowed from the face of the Crucified One and from the wound in His breast. Running down over the Host, these drops fell into the Chalice.

"Under the right arm of the cross was Our Lady with Her Immaculate Heart in Her hand ... She appeared as Our Lady of Fatima, with Her Immaculate Heart in Her left hand, without sword or roses, but with a crown of thorns and flames. Under the left arm of the cross, in large letters, like crystalline water which flowed over the altar, formed the words: 'Grace and Mercy.' I understood that the mystery of the Most Holy Trinity was shown to me, and I received lights about this mystery which I am not permitted to reveal. Then Our Lady said to me:

'The moment has come in which God asks the Holy Father to make, in union with all the bishops of the world, the consecration

of Russia to My Immaculate Heart, promising to save it by this means. So numerous are the souls which the justice of God condemns for sins committed against Me, that I come to ask for reparation. Sacrifice yourself for this intention and pray.'

"I rendered an account of this to my confessor, who ordered me to write down what Our Lord willed to be done."

On the 29th of October 1929 an overheated Wall Street finally crashed, a day which came to be known as Black Tuesday and which would mark the start of the Great Depression which lasted for ten long years.

While at Tuy, Lucia's confessor was Father Goncalves, and he had given her a list of questions that he hoped she could obtain answers for in the event of another apparition taking place. One of the questions was: "Why five Saturdays, and not nine, or seven, in honour of the sorrows of Our Lady?"

On the Feast of the Ascension, Thursday **29th May 1930**, Lucia was given the answer to this question, and she described that encounter with Jesus as follows:

"When I was in the chapel with Our Lord part of the night of May 29-30, 1930 and I spoke to Our Lord about questions four and five, I suddenly felt myself more intimately possessed by the Divine Presence and, if I am not mistaken, this is what was revealed to me:

'My daughter, the reason is simple. There are five types of offences and blasphemies committed against the Immaculate Heart of Mary:

Blasphemies against the Immaculate Conception.

Blasphemies against Her Perpetual Virginity.

Blasphemies against Her Divine Maternity, in refusing at the same time to recognise Her as the Mother of men.

The blasphemies of those who publicly seek to sow in the hearts of children indifference or scorn, or even hatred of this Immaculate Mother.

The offences of those who outrage Her directly in Her holy images.

'Here, My daughter, is the reason why the Immaculate Heart of Mary inspired Me to ask for this little act of Reparation ...'

'See, My daughter, the motive for which the Immaculate Heart of Mary inspired Me to ask for this little Reparation, and in consideration of it, to move My mercy to pardon souls who have had the misfortune of offending Her. As for you, always seek by your prayers and sacrifices to move My mercy to pity for these poor souls."'

There was a lengthy canonical enquiry into the apparitions and the Miracle of the Sun at Fatima, and finally on **13th October 1930**, the events at Fatima were declared 'worthy of belief' by Bishop da Silva, the Bishop of Leiria. This was seventeen years to the day, after the Miracle of the Sun was witnessed by tens of thousands of onlookers. Also in 1930, a papal indulgence was granted to all pilgrims visiting Fatima, but it's quite incredible that over two million people had already visited the town in the first ten years after the apparitions of 1917.

The next encounter Lucia had with Jesus was in **August 1931** at a chapel in Rianjo, near Pontevedra, where Lucia had been staying with her friend as she recovered from an illness. She subsequently wrote to her Bishop describing what Jesus had said regarding the consecration of Russia. In her letter, she wrote:

"Later, through an intimate communication, Our Lord complained to me: **'They did not wish to heed My request! ... Like the King of France they will repent of it, and they will do it, but it will be too late. Russia will have already spread its errors in the world, provoking wars and persecutions against the Church. The Holy Father will have much to suffer.'"**

It's thought that the reference to the King of France was referring to the revelation given to King Louis XIV by Margaret Mary Alacoque, that he should publically consecrate France to the Sacred Heart of Jesus. This revelation was given to Louis XIV on the 17th of June 1689, but he failed to comply with the request. The consecration was also not made by his son, Louis XV or by his grandson, Louis XVI when he came to power. One hundred years to the day after Margaret Mary Alacoque had made the request known to the King, and on the Feast of the Sacred Heart, 17th June 1789, the French Revolution began. Louis XVI was stripped of his legislative power by the National Assembly, and he was later guillotined on 21st January 1793. Marie Antoinette was also executed nine months later on 16th October 1793 at Place de la Concorde in Paris.

Margaret Mary was a Catholic nun and mystic who was ultimately canonised on 13th May 1920 by Pope Benedict XV. She was given several revelations over a period of 18 months from 27th December 1673, and three of the revelations were incorporated into Church practice. These are the devotion of receiving communion on the First Nine Fridays, the Eucharistic adoration during a holy hour on Thursdays, and the Feast of The Sacred Heart.

On the 30th of January 1933, Adolph Hitler became Chancellor of Germany, and just five weeks later on the 8th of March, the first concentration camp was opened at Dachau outside Munich. In May of that year there was a communal burning of Jewish and 'un-German' literature outside the Berlin Opera House. President Hindenburg died on the 2nd of August 1934, and Hitler then became Fuhrer of Germany on the 19th of that month.

Lucia took her final vows as a Dorothean sister in Tuy on 3rd October 1934, and Maria Rosa was there with her on this special day. This would be the last time she would see her mother, who passed away about eight years later on 16th July 1942, which is the feast date of Our Lady of Carmel.

At the third apparition at the Cova da Iria on 13th July 1917, Our Lady had said that if people did not cease offending God then a war worse than the current one (World War I) would break out. She said that the sign that this was about to happen would be the phenomenon of a night illumined by an unknown light. Amazingly, Our Lady even cited the name of the pope who would be head of the Church when this sign was given as being Pius XI. It's interesting that when Our Lady gave this prophecy in July 1917, Ambrogio Achille Ratti, who would later become Pope Pius XI, was just a lowly prefect of the library in the Vatican.

These were Our Lady's specific words on Friday 13th July 1917:

"You have seen hell where the souls of poor sinners go. To save them, God wishes to establish in the world devotion to my Immaculate

Heart. If what I say to you is done, many souls will be saved and there will be peace. The war is going to end; but if people do not cease offending God, a worse one will break out during the pontificate of Pius XI. When you see a night illumined by an unknown light, know that this is the great sign given you by God that He is about to punish the world for its crimes, by means of war, famine and persecutions of the Church and of the Holy Father.

"To prevent this, I shall come to ask for the consecration of Russia to my Immaculate Heart, and the Communion of Reparation on the First Saturdays. If my requests are heeded, Russia will be converted, and there will be peace; if not, she will spread her errors throughout the world, causing wars and persecutions of the Church. The good will be martyred, the Holy Father will have much to suffer, various nations will be annihilated.

"In the end, my Immaculate Heart will triumph. The Holy Father will consecrate Russia to me, and she will be converted, and a period of peace will be granted to the world. In Portugal, the dogma of the faith will always be preserved ..."

So Our Lady had offered two remedies to ensure peace and to prevent the outbreak of another World War. The first was the Devotion of the First Five Saturdays, and the specifics of this request were given to Lucia on 10th December 1925. On 13th July 1917, Our Lady had said that she would return to ask for the consecration of Russia to Her Immaculate Heart, and she did this on her appearance to Lucia on 13th June 1929. On this day, she specifically asked that this consecration be done by the Holy Father **in union with all the bishops of the world**.

Pius XI was elected to the papacy on the 6th of February 1922, and he held this office until his sudden death on the 10th of February 1939. In 1935, he had canonised Thomas More, four hundred years after his death. Thomas More had opposed the protestant theology of Martin Luther as well as King Henry VIII's split from the Catholic Church which resulted in More being tried for treason and then beheaded. Pius XI also canonised Don Bosco, who had started the Salesian Society for the care and education of orphans and deprived children. By the time of Don Bosco's death in 1888, there were 250 Salesian Houses catering for 130,000 children worldwide, and each year about 18,000 completed their apprenticeships.

- Chapter 6 -

Outbreak of World War II

In Germany, on 15th September 1935, two new racial laws were passed which came to be known as the Nuremberg Laws. These were the Reich Citizenship Law, and the Law to Protect German Blood and Honour, and the new legislation decreed that only Aryans could be full German citizens and it then became illegal for Aryans and Jews to marry. Fascism was also on the rise in both Italy and Spain, and civil war broke out in Spain on the 18th of July 1936. During this rise of fascism, Pius XI was outspoken in his criticism of Nazism in general, and specifically of Adolph Hitler and Benito Mussolini.

On the **25th of January 1938**, the spectacular warning that Our Lady had given of a night where the sky would be 'illumined by an unknown light' was seen throughout the whole of Europe. It was filmed, widely reported in the press and also detected by astronomical observatories throughout the continent.

Scientists described the phenomenon as an unusually brilliant Aurora Borealis, the most spectacular of the 20th century, and it was also differentiated from other Aurora Borealis events by how far south it extended. It was seen clearly in Sicily, in Gibraltar, and even in Madeira (32.6 degrees N).

Across the Atlantic, it was even visible in Bermuda (32.3 degrees N), and in the United States mainland it was observed as far south as San Diego in Southern California. The Aurora also disrupted radio signals all the way from Maine in the northeast of the US, to London.

This is how The Times newspaper reported the event the next day:

'A remarkable and very beautiful appearance of the Aurora Borealis, or Northern Lights, was seen last night from many parts of England, including the South, where the spectacle is seldom to be seen. The display began soon after sunset, and faded and recurred for varying periods over different areas of the country till a late hour. On the Downs of the South and West, on moors and hillsides in the North, on seaside cliffs, and on the higher ground of the outskirts of London, thousands of people gathered to watch the phenomenon. A pilot of an aeroplane crossing the channel circled a number of times at several thousand feet to give his passengers an unique opportunity of seeing it…'

The article continued: 'The glow, predominantly red in the sky as seen from parts of Sussex, suggested to many people, who left their homes at first in some alarm, the reflection of a great fire. From some points the phenomenon was observed continuously for some hours.'

The report ended with: 'A fisherman from Deal (Kent) who returned to port last night said: "It appeared as if the whole heavens were on fire, and great beams of red light, like steps, stretched across the sky."

Fire brigades were called out in Austria and Switzerland to attend to suspected fires, because the whole sky appeared as a flaming red curtain. In Budapest in Hungary the phenomenon lasted intermittently for about six hours and news reporters recorded the event in Munich and as far south as Gibraltar.

Fishermen in Ostend were so concerned about the significance of the phenomenon that they remained in port that night. Along the Pyrenees in villages near the frontier, the Aurora caused panic as the villagers thought that it was the result of an aerial bombardment in Spain.

Another newspaper reported: 'The Aurora, which has not been seen in Portugal for 50 years, was observed throughout the country for more than two-and-a-half hours.' It went on: 'Our Gibraltar correspondent states that the Aurora there took the form of streamers, arches, and patches of varying colour and shade, and offered a magnificent sight. It has not been seen at Gibraltar within living memory. The phenomenon was also visible in many districts of Italy, particularly Piedmont and Venetia. At Rome it appeared twice, and at Catania, in Sicily, three times.'

A correspondent in Vienna wrote: 'Yesterday's Aurora brought almost the whole population of Vienna into the streets, the cafés being emptied, while it lasted longer than at any time in living history.'

Just six weeks after this spectacular event, Hitler annexed Austria on 12th March 1938 and later that year he also annexed the Sudetenland border regions of Czechoslovakia. The land grab by Germany had begun and a new era of war which would have devastating consequences for the entire world was now on the horizon.

On the 9th and 10th of November 1938, thousands of Nazis attacked and burned hundreds of synagogues in Germany. Thousands of Jewish homes, schools and businesses were also attacked, and about one hundred Jews were killed in the night known as Kristallnacht, the night of broken glass. Shortly after this attack, about 30,000 Jewish men were arrested and taken to one of three Nazi concentration camps.

By 1939, Jews were not permitted to attend school or to hold public positions in either Germany or Italy, and they were also barred from working as lawyers or doctors. Pope Pius XI had been vociferous in his criticism of fascism and the appalling treatment of the Jews in Germany and Italy. He intended to make a stinging rebuke of Nazism and fascism with his Bishops in an encyclical he would pronounce on the 11th of February 1939, three months after Kristallnacht.

But by this time, reports had reached Mussolini that the pope may be about to excommunicate him, a move which would have severely damaged his (and Hitler's) support base in the general population. The Pope mysteriously died on 10th February 1939, the day before he was going to release the encyclical, apparently due to a heart attack.

He was buried in the grotto of Saint Peter's Basilica in the Apostolic Palace. The Pope had bravely stood up against Nazism and had defended the rights of the Jews right up until the day he died. He had indeed suffered much! Eugenio Pacelli, who was consecrated as a Bishop on 13th May 1917, the very day of the first apparition, was then elected to the papacy as Pius XII on the 2nd of March 1939.

On the **19th of March 1939**, a concerned Lucia wrote to the new pope:

"Whether the world has war or peace depends on the practice of this devotion, along with the consecration to the Immaculate Heart of Mary. This is why I desire its propagation so ardently, especially because this is also the will of our dear Mother in Heaven."

Lucia was clearly concerned that Our Lady's requests were still being ignored, and so on **20th June 1939** she wrote to Pius XII once again:

"Our Lady promised to put off the scourge of war, if this devotion was propagated and practiced. We see that She will obtain remission of this chastisement to the extent that efforts are made to propagate this devotion; but I fear that we can do more than we are doing and that God, being displeased, will pull back the arm of His mercy and let the world be ravaged by this chastisement which will be unlike any other in the past, horrible, horrible."

On **1st September 1939**, Germany invaded Poland, even though Britain had an alliance with that country in which she guaranteed her independence. Britain issued an ultimatum to end hostilities, and when this was ignored, Britain declared war on Germany on 3rd September. The Soviet Union, which had signed the Molotov-Ribbentrop Pact with Germany on 23rd August, invaded Poland from the East, on 17th September. This non-aggression pact had a secret protocol within it, which would see different parts of Europe split into German and Soviet spheres of influence in the event of war breaking out.

Our Lady had asked for the Holy Father to consecrate Russia to her Immaculate Heart in an apparition at Tuy on 13th June 1929. On that visit, she had again asked for reparation to be made for the sins committed against her Immaculate Heart - the Communion of Reparation on the First Five Saturdays. This was ten years before the outbreak of World War II.

Lucia said that when Our Lord had appeared to her at the chapel in Rianjo in August 1931, He had complained that they had still not acted on Our Lady's requests, and He had warned of the consequences of this. Lucia played her part and immediately wrote to her bishop advising him of the revelation she had received. Unfortunately, Our Lady's requests were still ignored, and World War II had now begun.

On the 2nd of December 1940, Lucia wrote to Pius XII once again, regarding Our Lady's request for Russia to be consecrated to Her Immaculate Heart. Lucia was clearly concerned that all her requests for this consecration to be made, and for the First Five Saturdays devotion to be adopted, had not been actioned by the Church.

By now, Germany and Russia had occupied Poland, and Germany had defeated France, Denmark, Finland, Norway, Belgium, Luxembourg, Holland, Czechoslovakia and Romania. On the 10th of May 1940, Winston Churchill had become Prime Minister, and one month later, on the 10th of June, Italy also declared war on Britain.

On the 10th of July of that year, the Battle of Britain began. This was the largest aerial battle in history, and resulted in the loss of about 1023 British fighter planes and 1887 German bombers and fighters. Some

544 British pilots and 2500 German aircrew were killed in the battle, which raged until the end of October 1940, and the Blitz of London would kill about 40,000 civilians.

The war in North Africa was also underway, as well as the Battle for the Atlantic, with massive numbers of German U-Boats attacking naval vessels and supply ships. These were dark days indeed for the world and it's no wonder that Lucia felt it necessary to appeal yet again to the pope, to action Our Lady's requests. She wrote:

'Most Holy Father,

'Humbly prostrated at your feet, I come as the last sheep of the fold entrusted to you to open my heart, by order of my spiritual director.

'I am the only survivor of the children to whom our Lady appeared in Fátima (Portugal) from the 13th of May to the 13th of October 1917. The Blessed Virgin has granted me many graces, the greatest of all being my admission to the Institute of Saint Dorothy.

'I come, Most Holy Father, to renew a request that has already been brought to you several times. The request, Most Holy Father, is from our Lord and our good Mother in Heaven.

'In 1917, in the portion of the apparitions that we have designated 'the secret,' the Blessed Virgin revealed the end of the war that was then afflicting Europe, and predicted another forthcoming, saying that to prevent it She would come and ask the consecration of Russia to Her Immaculate Heart as well as the Communion of reparation on the first Saturdays. She promised peace and the conversion of that nation if Her request was attended to.

'She announced that otherwise this nation would spread her errors throughout the world, and there would be wars, persecutions of the Holy Church, martyrdom of many Christians, several persecutions and sufferings reserved for Your Holiness, and the annihilation of several nations.

'Most Holy Father, this remained a secret until 1926 according to the express will of our Lady. Then, in a revelation She asked that the Communion of reparation on the first Saturdays of five consecutive months be propagated throughout the world, with its conditions of doing the following with the same purpose; going to confession, meditating for a quarter of an hour on the mysteries of the rosary and saying the rosary with the aim of making reparation for the insults, sacrileges and indifferences committed against Her Immaculate Heart.

'Our good Heavenly Mother promises to assist the persons who practice this devotion, in the hour of their death, with all the necessary graces for their salvation. I exposed the request of our Lady to my confessor, who tried to have it fulfilled, but only on the 13th of September 1939 did His Excellency the Bishop of Leiria make public in Fatima this request of Our Lady.

'I take this opportunity, Most Holy Father, to ask you to bless and extend this devotion to the whole world. In 1929, through another apparition, our Lady asked for the consecration of Russia to Her Immaculate Heart, promising its conversion through this means and the hindering of the propagation of its errors.

'Sometime afterwards I told my confessor of the request of our Lady. He tried to fulfill it by making it known to Pius XI.

'In several intimate communications our Lord has not stopped insisting on this request, promising lately, to shorten the days of tribulation which He has determined to punish the nations for their crimes, through war, famine and several persecutions of the Holy Church and Your Holiness, if you will consecrate the world to the Immaculate Heart of Mary, with a special mention for Russia, and order that all the Bishops of the world do the same in union with Your Holiness.

'I truly feel your sufferings, Most Holy Father! And, as much as I can through my humble prayers and sacrifices, I try to lessen them, close to our Lord and the Immaculate Heart of Mary.

'Most Holy Father, if in the union of my soul with God I have not been deceived, our Lord promises a special protection to our country in this war, due to the consecration of the nation by the Portuguese Prelates, to the Immaculate Heart of Mary; as proof of the graces that would have been granted to other nations, had they also consecrated themselves to Her.

'Now, Most Holy Father, allow me to make one more request, which is but an ardent wish of my humble heart; that the feast in honour of the Immaculate Heart of Mary be extended throughout the whole world as one of the main feasts of the Holy Church.

'With the deepest respect and reverence I ask for the Apostolic Blessing. May God protect Your Holiness.

Tuy, Spain, **2nd of December of 1940**. Maria Lucia de Jesus.'

In June 1938, while Pius XI was still alive, there had been a request for him to consecrate the world (as opposed to Russia specifically) to the Immaculate Heart of Mary.

But this time the request for consecration didn't come from Lucia, but from a Jesuit priest, Father Mariano Pinho, and several Portuguese bishops. The request was as a result of messages that a lady named Alexandrina Maria da Costa, from Balazar in Portugal, said she had received from Jesus and the Virgin Mary.

When Alexandrina was fourteen years of age, four men had attempted to break into her room to attack her, and to escape she had jumped out of a window, falling thirteen feet to the ground. Her spine was broken and she suffered from a deteriorating paralysis that later confined her to bed for thirty years, from 1925 until her death on the 13th of October 1955.

According to her Vatican biography, Alexandrina received no food except the Holy Eucharist each day from March 1942 onwards. Miraculously, she survived without food for thirteen years! The request by Father Pinho and the Portuguese Bishops was made several times through to 1941 when Pius XII was in office, and the Vatican on three occasions requested additional information about Alexandrina. Pope John Paul II would later declare Alexandrina of Balazar 'blessed' on the 25th of April 2004.

On the morning of Sunday 7th December 1941, Japan launched an unprovoked attack on ships of the US Pacific Fleet stationed at Pearl Harbor in Oahu, Hawaii. Japan then attacked US bases in the Philippines and Guam, and the British-controlled territories of Borneo, Malaya, Singapore and Hong Kong. The next day, Britain declared war on Japan, and the US Congress voted to go to war with Japan nine hours later. Germany and Italy subsequently declared war on the United States, bringing her fully into World War II.

On the **13th of May 1942**, the 25th anniversary of the first apparition, the Vatican finally published 'The Message and Secret of Fatima.'

However, this did not include details of the 'third secret,' which Lucia had kept to herself.

Finally, thirteen years and four months after Our Lady's request at Tuy, and three whole years into World War II, Pope Pius XII did make a consecration to the Immaculate Heart of Mary.

In his radio address in Portuguese on **31st October 1942**, the Pope consecrated the Church and all of humanity to the Immaculate Heart of Mary, with specific mention of Russia. This is a small part of his address:

"To you, to your Immaculate Heart, we as common Father of the great Christian family, as Vicar of the One who was given all power in Heaven and on Earth, received the request of many souls redeemed with His Blood who populate the world, - to You, to Your Immaculate Heart, at this tragic time of human history we trust, we deliver, consecrate not only the Holy Church, the mystical body of Jesus, that pities and bleeds into so many pieces and by so many ways troubled, but also the entire world, torn by discord, scorched in fires of hatred, a victim of its own iniquities."

However, Lucia later commented that the consecration by Pius XII was not in accord with what Our Lady had requested as it lacked the participation of all the bishops of the Church.

In June 1943, Lucia fell seriously ill which greatly concerned Bishop da Silva and so in October of that year after Lucia had recovered, Canon Galamba, an advisor to the bishop, suggested that he ask Lucia to commit her vision of 13th July 1917 (the third secret) to writing. Canon Galamba advised the bishop to ask Lucia to place the text in an envelope sealed with wax, but only to be opened at a later date.

The bishop clearly had concerns that should Lucia die suddenly then the third secret would die with her and so he personally went to Tuy on 15th September 1943 with his request. Lucia then asked if the bishop could put his instruction in writing, which he subsequently did in mid-October.

Lucia was agonising over what to do for several weeks, but she had another visitation by Our Lady on **2nd January 1944** to reassure her that this was indeed the will of God. Lucia subsequently wrote to

Bishop da Silva on the 9th of January 1944 to advise him that she had complied with his request.

She wrote, "I have written what you asked me; God willed to try me a little, but finally, this was indeed His will: it (the third part of the Secret) is sealed in an envelope and it is in the notebooks…"

This clearly implies that the account of the vision was written down twice i.e. in the letter in the sealed envelope and also in her notebooks. Lucia had kept the vision she was given on 13th July 1917 a secret for 26 years, but it was still to remain a secret for a very long time to come!

Lucia hand-delivered the envelope to Bishop Ferreira, the Archbishop of Gurza, who gave it that same evening to Bishop da Silva. However the letter remained unopened at this time and it was agreed that if Bishop da Silva were to die, then the envelope would be given to Cardinal Cerejeira, the Patriarch of Lisbon.

Lucia had written on the envelope that it could only be opened **after 1960**, either by the Patriarch of Lisbon or by the Bishop of Leiria.

The war in Europe ended with the surrender of Germany on the 7th of May 1945, and hostilities ended in the East with the surrender of Japan on the 2nd of September of that year. The war had directly killed about 60 million people, or 2.5% of the world population. In addition to this, another 19 to 25 million had died from war-related famine and disease, and so the overall figure was between 79 and 85 million deaths. Of this total, civilian casualties are estimated to have been at least 38 million.

World War II saw the use of biological weapons, when Japan dropped clay bombs, each containing 30,000 bubonic plague infected fleas, on Quzhou in China in October 1940. This killed over 2000 people in the town, but many more died when the plague spread further afield. Japanese forces also poisoned over 1000 water wells with cholera, and they employed the deadly anthrax bacteria in Zhejiang Province in 1942. This war also saw the use of nuclear weapons for the first time, with combined deaths at Hiroshima and Nagasaki estimated at a minimum of 150,000, with the higher estimates being around 244,000.

Our Lady had warned us of the horror of this war, and she had given mankind a remedy to prevent it, but the world had simply not responded to her pleas.

- Chapter 7 -
Third secret remains a secret

Although the war had ended in 1945, the world would soon see the start of the Cold War, and as Our Lady had warned in 1917, Russia would spread her errors throughout the world. After the conflict in Europe had ended, the Soviet Union defiantly refused to cede control of the parts of Germany that it had occupied during the conflict.

This resulted in the creation of the Federal Republic of Germany, commonly called West Germany, when Britain, the US, and France amalgamated the parts of Germany they had captured in 1945. The city of Berlin was also split into four sectors controlled by the US, Britain, France, and the Soviet Union.

On the 25th of March 1948, Lucia dos Santos entered the Carmelite Convent in Coimbra, and here she assumed the name, Sister Maria Lucia of the Immaculate Heart.

A few years later, on the 13th of October 1951, Cardinal Tedeschini who was the Papal Legate, made the most incredible announcement. He said in his address to a crowd of one million people who were gathered at Fatima that Pius XII had personally witnessed a repetition of the 1917 Miracle of the Sun while he was in the Vatican gardens.

The Pope had witnessed this event not once, but four times, on 30th October, 31st October, 1st November and 8th November 1950. The Pope had promulgated the dogma of the Corporal Assumption of the Blessed Virgin Mary on the 1st of November 1950, and he took this miracle as confirmation that his intention to do so was correct.

The Pope was deeply affected by what he'd seen, and he spoke about the solar phenomena with some of his cardinals and close colleagues. Sister Lehnert, who was in charge of the papal apartments at the time, said: "Pius XII was very convinced of the reality of the extraordinary phenomenon, which he had seen on four occasions."

On 30th April 1952, Bishop Jose da Silva, of the Diocese of Leiria, initiated the first stage in the process that would lead to the beatification of Francisco and Jacinta Marto. The diocesan phase gathers detailed information on the candidate for sainthood, and looks for evidence of heroic virtue in the person's observance of the Gospel.

This process can take many years, and if the candidate is categorically shown to have displayed heroic virtue in their life, then the pope will make a solemn proclamation that the person really did live as a saint and deserves to be held up as an example to follow. However, before making this declaration, the Church requires evidence of a miracle that was obtained through the intercession of the candidate for sainthood.

In the case of Jacinta and Francisco, the first phase would take over 27 years, mainly because of an ongoing theological debate in the Church over whether or not pre-adolescent children could be canonised. In 1937, Pope Pius XI had decided that causes for minors should not be accepted as they could not fully understand heroic virtue, or practice it repeatedly.

About a year and eight months after witnessing the solar phenomenon in the Vatican gardens, Pope Pius XII consecrated Russia to the Blessed Virgin Mary. This was in his Apostolic letter, 'Sacro Vergente Anno' of **7th July 1952**. The relevant text is:

"And therefore we, in order that our and your prayers may be more easily answered, and in order to give you a special attestation of our benevolence, in the same way as a few years ago we consecrated the entire world to the immaculate Heart of the virgin Mother of God, so now, in a very special way, consecrate all peoples of Russia to the very same immaculate Heart, in the safe confidence that with the extremely powerful protection of the virgin Mary the wishes expressed by us, by you and by every good person for a true peace for fraternal concord and due freedom for everyone and for the Church in the first place, may be answered as soon as possible; in such a manner that, through the prayer that we send up to Heaven together with you and all Christians, the reign of Christ, harbinger of salvation, which is 'kingdom of truth and life, kingdom of sainthood and grace, kingdom of justice, of love and of peace', may triumph and steadily consolidate itself everywhere on earth."

However this entrustment also didn't satisfy the condition that it should be made 'in union with all the bishops of the world' as Our Lady clearly wanted this consecration of Russia to be made by the entire Church on Earth and not just by the pontiff himself.

It was also in 1952 that Soviet forces erected a barbed wire fence between East and West Germany in an attempt to stop mass emigration to the West, but citizens living in the Soviet-controlled sector of Berlin were still able to cross into the sectors controlled by the United States, Britain and France.

In 1956 there was simmering unrest in Hungary against the Marxist government with its Soviet-imposed policies, and this finally erupted into the Hungarian Revolution of 23rd October to 10th November of that year. The revolution began with benign student demonstrations, when a peaceful crowd of 20,000 gathered outside the Parliament Buildings in Budapest. But the students then began chanting a freedom song with the refrain, "This we swear, this we swear, that we will no longer be slaves."

The students were soon joined by many thousands of workers until a crowd of some 200,000 had taken to the streets of the capital. They toppled the 30 foot high statue of Stalin, with some of the students then occupying the Radio Budapest building in an attempt to voice their demands to the government in a radio address before the nation.

The State Security Police arrested them, but the real flashpoint came when the police shot into the crowd, killing one of the students. The protesters wrapped the lifeless body in a flag and then carried it into the air above their heads. The Hungarian flag, with the Communist coat of arms cut out of the centre of it then became the symbol of the revolt. 31,000 Soviet troops and 1130 tanks soon poured into Budapest to subdue the uprising but the brave revolutionaries fought back with Molotov cocktails and small arms and it took two-and-a-half weeks of bitter fighting to subdue them. But the failed attempt to win back their freedom had come at a high cost, and at the end of the fighting, 2,500 Hungarians lay dead, with another 20,000 injured.

It was in early 1957 while Pius XII was still in office that the Vatican requested that the envelope Lucia had given to Bishop da Silva on the 17th of June 1944, her notebooks, and copies of all her writings that were being held at the Chancery of Leiria, be sent through to the Papal nuncio. Bishop da Silva later gave these documents to his auxiliary Bishop, Venancio in the middle of March 1957. Venancio then took them to Bishop Cento, who was the Apostolic Nuncio to Lisbon. Lucia's letter and the other documents finally arrived at the Vatican on the **16th of April 1957**, and were then placed in a little chest in the office of Pius XII.

Eight months later, on the **26th of December 1957**, Lucia was interviewed by Father Augustine Fuentes at her convent in Coimbra, and this is part of what she said to him that day:

"The Blessed Virgin is very sad, for no one attaches any importance to Her Message, neither the good nor the bad. The good continue on their way but without giving any importance to Her Message. The bad, not seeing the punishment of God actually falling upon them, continue their life of sin without even caring about the message. But believe me Father, God will chastise the world and this will be in a terrible manner. The punishment from heaven is imminent."

Given that Lucia made this statement twelve years after World War II had ended, it's clear that she was still deeply concerned that the world would be subjected to yet another terrible chastisement if Our Lady's requests were not actioned. (Father Fuentes was postulator of the beatification causes of Jacinta and Francisco.)

It's impossible to say whether or not Pope Pius XII ultimately intended to make the third secret known to the world. After all, he did have the envelope in his possession at the Vatican for 18 months without releasing it by the time of his death on the 9th of October 1958. Apparently, the envelope was never even opened by the pope.

Pius XII, who always had a special relationship with Our Lady, was laid to rest in the crypt of Saint Peter's Basilica on the 13th of October, which fittingly is the feast date of Our Lady of Fatima, as well as the date on which the Miracle of the Sun occurred.

John XXIII then took the papacy on the 28th of October 1958, and on the **17th of August 1959**, the pope requested the envelope containing the third secret. The envelope was taken to him at Castel Gandolfo by Monsignor Philippe, a Vatican official. Castel Gandolfo is a 17th century papal palace in the town of the same name, and is situated about 24 kilometres southeast of Rome.

Castel Gandolfo has had an interesting history, with popes often using it as a retreat, but during World War II it gave sanctuary to a very large number of Jewish refugees who were escaping the Nazis. Under the

Lateran Treaty of 1929, it was protected as an extraterritorial property of the Holy See. Both Pius XII and Paul VI died at Castel Gandolfo.

For some reason, John XXIII didn't read the letter that same day but only opened it a few days later and the Portuguese text was translated for the pontiff by Monsignor Paulo Jose Tavarez. The pope also asked that it be read to Cardinal Ottaviani, who was the Prefect of the Holy Office at that time.

By 1960, the public were expecting the third secret to finally be revealed, but about six months after John XXIII had read the contents of Lucia's letter, a press statement by the Vatican was released on the **8th February 1960**:

'Faced with the pressure that has been placed on the Vatican, some wanting the letter to be opened and made known to the world, others, on the supposition that it may contain alarming prophecies, desiring that its publication be withheld, the same Vatican circles declare that the Vatican has decided not to make public Sister Lucia's letter, and to continue keeping it rigorously sealed.

'The decision of the Vatican authorities is based on various reasons: 1. Sister Lucia is still living. 2. The Vatican already knows the contents of the letter. 3. Although the Church recognises the Fatima apparitions, she does not pledge herself to guarantee the veracity of the words which the three little shepherds claim to have heard from Our Lady. In these circumstances, it is most probable that the Secret of Fatima will remain, forever, under absolute seal.'

Between 1949 and 1961, over two-and-a-half million East Germans had managed to flee to the West, and so on 13th August 1961, East German forces erected a barbed wire fence between the Soviet sector and the Allied sectors of Berlin. Two days later, construction of the massive concrete Berlin Wall began.

On 11th October 1962, John XXIII convened the Second Vatican Council. It was actually the 21st Ecumenical Council, but only the second council to be held at St Peter's Basilica, and it essentially addressed the relations between the Catholic Church and the modern world. One of the most profound changes introduced was permission to say the mass in the vernacular instead of Latin.

By now, the Cold War was now entering a highly dangerous phase and this culminated in the Cuban Missile Crisis of 16th to 28th October 1962. The Soviet leader, Nikita Khrushchev had agreed to a secret request from Fidel Castro to deploy ballistic missiles in Cuba and construction of the launch sites began in the summer of 1962.

When a US spy plane captured images of short and medium-range ballistic missile sites on the island, it resulted in a blockade by the US Navy. After 13 days of high tension, Khrushchev finally agreed to the removal of the missiles, and John F. Kennedy gave an undertaking that the US would not attempt an invasion of Cuba, and he also agreed to the dismantling of ballistic missiles that had been deployed in Turkey.

Pope John XXIII died on the 3rd of June 1963 in the Apostolic Palace of the Vatican City, and then Paul VI took office on the 21st of June. The following year, on the **21st of November 1964**, Paul VI renewed the consecration of the whole world to the Immaculate Heart of Mary. This was done with the Bishops present at the close of the third session of the Second Vatican Council but it was not done with their participation, and again Russia was not specifically named in the consecration. In his address, the Pope proclaimed Mary as Mother of the Church, and he also placed the whole Church under the protection of Our Lady of Fatima.

Paul VI read the text of the third secret on **27th of March 1965** in the presence of Archbishop Angelo Dell'Acqua but he also decided not to publish its contents and he then returned the letter to the Vatican archives. However, the pontiff did endorse official Church support for Fatima by making his own pilgrimage there on the 13th of May 1967. This was the 50th anniversary of the first apparition, and he prayed together with Lucia at the shrine.

Pope Paul VI died on the 6th of August 1978, and was succeeded by John Paul I (born Albino Luciani) who only held the papacy for just 33 days until his death at the age of sixty-five on the 28th of September 1978. John Paul I was the first Pope to take a double name, and the first to do away with the coronation ceremony for a new pope.

Bishop Jose da Silva of Leiria had initiated the diocesan phase for the beatification of Francisco and Jacinta on 30th April 1952, but as the Church hadn't changed its stance on non-martyred, pre-adolescent children becoming saints, the documentation had still not been forwarded through to Rome.

So in 1979, Alberto Cosme do Amaral, who was the Bishop of Leiria at the time, asked all the bishops of the world to petition John Paul II to make an exception in the case of Francisco and Jacinta. The Congregation for the Causes of Saints subsequently received a flood of letters from 30 cardinals, 25 archbishops and 195 bishops arguing that children should be eligible for canonisation and asking for the cause of Francisco and Jacinta to be allowed to proceed.

The Congregation for the Causes of Saints then convened a general assembly of theologians, cardinals and bishops to debate the issue of whether it was possible for children to display heroic virtue, and they concluded that it was indeed possible.

The documentation on Francisco and Jacinta was then forwarded to Rome on 2nd June 1979, finally closing the diocesan stage of the process, but before beatification, it would be necessary for a miracle to be attributed to the children's intercession.

- Chapter 8 -
The consecration of Russia

On Wednesday **13th May 1981**, the anniversary of the first apparition at Fatima, there was an assassination attempt on Pope John Paul II as he was being driven slowly through a crowd of 20,000 people standing in an open car in St Peter's Square at 5:15 in the afternoon. Four shots were fired from very close range, about 15 feet, and the Pope was hit in his lower intestine, right arm, and left index finger. The 9mm bullets from the Browning pistol caused severe blood loss necessitating a transfusion of 6 pints of blood, and parts of the pope's intestine had to be removed in three places. Doctor Rodolfo Proietti, the chief physician who operated on the pope for five hours and twenty-five minutes said, "I don't know how he survived the shooting."

The shooter, Mehmet Ali Agca was sentenced to life, but was later forgiven by the pope, who famously went to visit him in prison in 1983. He was later pardoned by the Italian President Carlo Ciampi at the pope's request, and then deported to Turkey in June 2000. The pope would later give one of the bullets which so nearly claimed his life, to the Bishop of Leiria-Fatima on his visit to Rome. The Bishop then had the bullet set in the crown of the statue of Our Lady in the shrine at Fatima.

As the pope was recovering from his injuries, he wrote an Act of Entrustment which he wanted to be announced to the world in the Basilica of Saint Mary Major on the **7th of June 1981**, and as he was unable to be physically present his recorded address was broadcast instead. The part of the entrustment that clearly related to Russia, although it was not specifically mentioned by name, is given below:

'Mother of all individuals and peoples, you know all their sufferings and hopes. In your motherly heart you feel all the struggles between good and evil, between light and darkness, that convulse the world: accept the plea which we make in the Holy Spirit directly to your heart, and embrace with the love of the Mother and Handmaid of the Lord those who most await this embrace, and also **those whose act of entrustment you too await in a particular way.** Take under your motherly protection the whole human family, which with affectionate love we entrust to you, O Mother. May there dawn for everyone the time of peace and freedom, the time of truth, of justice and of hope.'

John Paul II was absolutely convinced that Our Lady had intervened to save his life and so he then asked that Lucia's letter be brought to him. On **18th July 1981**, the pontiff was given two envelopes - a white one containing the original Portuguese text, and an orange envelope containing an Italian translation of the text. It was Archbishop Martinez Somalo, Substitute of the Secretariat of State, who handed him the envelopes. Later, on the 11th of August, Archbishop Somalo returned the envelopes to the Vatican Archives.

Lucia wrote to John Paul II on the **12th of May 1982**, and in her letter she explained that the fulfillment of **some** of the warnings in the prophecies given on the 13th of July 1917 had already come about. She wrote that 'this had happened because mankind had not responded to Our Lady's requests.' Furthermore, Lucia warned that we may well be moving towards the fulfillment of the **final part of the prophecy** due to the prevalence of so much sin in the world.

We must bear in mind that Lucia's letter was written **after** the assassination attempt on John Paul II. In other words, the assassination attempt was not the end point of the prophecy in the third secret, otherwise she would not have written:

'And if we have not yet seen the **complete fulfillment of the final part of this prophecy**, we are going towards it little by little with great strides.'

These are Lucia's words in her letter of 12th May 1982 to John Paul II:

'The third part of the secret refers to Our Lady's words: 'If not, Russia will spread her errors throughout the world, causing wars and persecutions of the Church. The good will be martyred; the Holy Father will have much to suffer; various nations will be annihilated' (13-VII-1917).

'The third part of the secret is a symbolic revelation, referring to this part of the Message, conditioned by whether we accept or not what the Message itself asks of us: 'If my requests are heeded, Russia will be converted, and there will be peace; if not, she will spread her errors throughout the world, etc.'

'Since we did not heed this appeal of the Message, we see that it has been fulfilled, Russia has invaded the world with her errors. And if we have not yet seen the complete fulfillment of the final part of this prophecy, we are going towards it little by little with great strides. If we do not reject the path of sin, hatred, revenge, injustice, violations of the rights of the human person, immorality and violence, etc.

'And let us not say that it is God who is punishing us in this way; on the contrary it is people themselves who are preparing their own punishment. In his kindness God warns us and calls us to the right path, while respecting the freedom he has given us; hence people are responsible.'

The day after Lucia wrote this letter, and exactly a year to the day after the assassination attempt, the pope visited Fatima on the **13th of May 1982**.

The pope explained to the great crowd that had gathered why he had visited Fatima by saying, **"On this exact date last year in St Peter's Square in Rome, there was an attempt on the life of your Pope, which mysteriously coincided with the anniversary of the first vision at Fatima, that of 13 May 1917. The coincidence of these dates was so great that it seemed to be a special invitation for me to come here."**

After a concelebrated mass, Pope John Paul II consecrated the whole world to the Immaculate Heart of Mary. This is part of his address:

'Forty years ago and again ten years later, your servant Pope Pius XII, having before his eyes the painful experience of the human family, entrusted and consecrated to your Immaculate Heart the whole world, especially the peoples for which you had particular love and solicitude. This world of individuals and nations I too have before my eyes today, as I renew the entrusting and consecration carried out by my Predecessor in the See of Peter: the world of the second millennium that is drawing to a close, the modern world, our world today!

'The Church, mindful of the Lord's words: 'Go... and make disciples of all nations... and lo, I am with you always, to the close of the age', renewed at the Second Vatican Council her awareness of her mission in this world.

'And therefore, O Mother of individuals and peoples, you who 'know all their sufferings - and their hopes', you who have a mother's awareness of all the struggles between good and evil, between light and darkness, which afflict the modern world, accept the cry which we, as though moved by the Holy Spirit, address directly to your Heart. Embrace, with the love of the Mother and Handmaid, this human world of ours, which we entrust and consecrate to you, for we are full of disquiet for the earthly and eternal destiny of individuals and peoples. In a special way we entrust and consecrate to you those individuals and **nations which particularly need to be entrusted and consecrated.** We have recourse to your protection, holy Mother of God: reject not the prayers we send up to you in our necessities.'

The Pope ended his address with these words which specifically covered the areas of war, including nuclear war, abortion, injustice in society and atheism.

'In entrusting to you, O Mother, the world, all individuals and peoples, we also entrust to you the consecration itself, for the world's sake, placing it in your motherly Heart.

Oh, Immaculate Heart! Help us to conquer the menace of evil, which so easily takes root in the hearts of the people of today, and whose immeasurable effects already weigh down upon our modern world and seem to block the paths towards the future!

From famine and war, deliver us.

From nuclear war, from incalculable self-destruction, from every kind of war, deliver us.

From sins against the life of man from its very beginning, deliver us.

From hatred and from the demeaning of the dignity of the children of God, deliver us.

From every kind of injustice in the life of society, both national and international, deliver us.

From readiness to trample on the commandments of God, deliver us.

From attempts to stifle in human hearts the very truth of God, deliver us.

From sins against the Holy Spirit, deliver us, deliver us.

Accept, O Mother of Christ, this cry laden with the sufferings of all individual human beings, laden with the sufferings of whole societies.

'Let there be revealed, once more in the history of the world your infinite power of merciful Love. May it put a stop to evil. May it transform consciences. May your Immaculate Heart reveal for all the light of Hope.'

Although Russia was again not mentioned specifically, the words 'In a special way we entrust and consecrate to you those individuals and nations which particularly need to be entrusted and consecrated' were clearly referring to Russia. The pope had in fact invited all the bishops to join him in this consecration but many had not received the invitation by the 13th of May 1982 and so the consecration had still not involved the participation of all of the world's bishops, and again Sister Lucia said that it did not fulfill the request of Our Lady.

During his homily at the mass he celebrated on that day, the pope said:

"The Message is addressed to every human being. ... Because of the continuing increase of sin and the dangers, such as nuclear war, now threatening humanity, the Message of Fatima is more urgent and relevant in our time than it was when Our Lady appeared 65 years ago."

He also said: "Today John Paul II, successor of St. Peter, presents himself before the Mother of the Son of God in Her shrine at Fatima. In what way does he come? He presents himself reading again with trepidation the motherly call to penance, to conversion, the ardent appeal of the Heart of Mary that resounded at Fatima 65 years ago. Yes he reads it again with trepidation in his heart because he sees how many people and societies - how many Christians - have gone in the opposite direction to the one indicated in the Message of Fatima. Sin has thus made itself firmly at home in the world, and denial of God has become widespread in the ideologies, ideas and plans of human beings."

Finally, on the **25th of March 1984**, John Paul II renewed the 1982 consecration that he had made at Fatima, and this time the bishops had all been notified that their participation was required well in advance. The pope had requested that the statue of Our Lady of Fatima be brought through to Rome for this special occasion. This was the feast of the Annunciation and the Pope made the consecration on his knees before the statue of Our Lady of Fatima, which is the same statue that is now venerated in the Chapel of the Apparitions.

Again, the text didn't mention Russia specifically, but the Pope did reference the acts of consecration made by Pope Pius XII in 1942 and 1952, and the 1952 consecration was essentially concerned with Russia. It also appears that John Paul II paused at times during the ceremony, and according to the Bishop of Leiria-Fatima, Alberto Cosme do Amaral, he quietly included Russia in the consecration wording.

But what of Our Lady's other request – the establishment of a devotion to Her Immaculate Heart through the Communion of Reparation on the First Five Saturdays? Unfortunately, it's clear that the world has virtually ignored this request of Our Lady.

On 13th May 1989, the 72nd anniversary of the first apparition at Fatima, Pope John Paul II issued a decree declaring Jacinta and Francisco 'venerable' and this was a formal recognition that the two children had lived out their Christian lives in a heroic way.

Three months earlier, a woman named Maria Emilia Santos from Leiria in Portugal, claimed that she'd been miraculously healed after praying to Jacinta and Francisco Marto. Emilia's spinal column had been calcified, rendering her bed-ridden and unable to walk for 22 years, 8 of which were spent in hospital before she was placed in the Institute of St Francis, a home for people suffering from severe chronic illnesses. Emilia continually prayed for a cure, including making novenas and asking for the intercession of Francisco and Jacinta.

On the evening of 20th February 1989, the anniversary date of Jacinta's death, as she was lying flat on her bed reflecting on the saint's life and praying to her, she suddenly realised that she could move her feet and even bend her spine. Astonished by this, she placed her feet on the ground and was shocked to discover that she could sense the cold floor for the very first time.

Emilia pushed on the bed with her hands and was then able to get into a standing position. She took one step, and then another, crying with joy as she realised that she was able to walk. Another patient in the home saw Emilia walking, and began shouting for the assistants, who rushed into the room and then stood there looking at her in disbelief.

The following day, the doctors who had been treating Emilia went to the home to examine her, repeating the word 'impossible' over and over again, with one of them exclaiming, "Nothing in human science could have brought about this cure!"

However, the verification of a miracle by the Catholic Church is a lengthy and meticulous process, split into two investigations. The first is a scientific examination of the healing by a commission of doctors, to decide if the cure cannot be explained in scientific terms. A second investigation, by a commission of theologians, establishes whether the intervention was brought about solely through the intercession of the candidate for sainthood. The investigations can take years to reach a conclusion, and the case involving Emilia would take over 10 years.

Debate continues to this day as to whether or not the 25th of March 1984 consecration satisfied the conditions set out by Our Lady. However the Apostolic Nuncio visited Sister Lucia after this consecration and she is reported to have confirmed that the 1984 consecration did indeed satisfy the request of Our Lady. In October 1989, an interview with Sister Lucia was published in the Fatima Family Messenger, and in it she said that the Apostolic Nuncio had asked her, "Is Russia now consecrated?"

Lucia said that she had replied to the interviewer, "Yes, now it is."

Then Lucia was asked, "Now we wait for the miracle?" to which she replied, "God will keep His word."

Lucia also wrote another letter on the 8th of November 1989, which was subsequently published in the March 1990 edition of the Catholic publication '30 days.' Regarding the consecration of Russia, she wrote:

"It was later made by the present Pontiff, John Paul II, on 25th March 1984, after he wrote to all the Bishops of the World, asking that each of them make the consecration in his own diocese with the people of God who had been entrusted to him. The Pope asked that the statue of Our Lady of Fatima be brought to Rome and he did it publicly in union with all the bishops who, with His Holiness, were uniting themselves with the people of God, the Mystical Body of Christ; and it was made to the Immaculate Heart of Mary, Mother of Christ and of His mystical body, so that, with her and through her with Christ, the consecration could be carried and offered to the Father for the salvation of humanity. Thus the consecration was made by His Holiness Pope John Paul II on 25th March 1984."

The next year, on the 3rd of July 1990, Lucia wrote a letter to Father Robert J. Fox, and in it she again confirmed that Our Lady's request regarding the consecration of Russia had been achieved.

She wrote: "I come to answer your question, 'If the consecration made by Pope John Paul II on March 25, 1984 in union with all the bishops of the world, accomplished the conditions for the consecration of Russia according to the request of Our Lady in Tuy on June 13 of 1929?' Yes, it was accomplished, and since then I have said that it was made. And I say that no other person responds for me, it is I who receive and open all letters and respond to them."

Archbishop Tarcisio Bertone also issued a statement in 2001 claiming that during a meeting with Sister Lucia on the 17th of November of that year, she had told him, "I have already said that the consecration desired by Our Lady was made in 1984, and has been accepted in Heaven."

Tarcisio Bertone was at that time the Secretary of the Congregation for the Doctrine of the Faith. Sister Lucia was ninety-four at the time, and the meeting was conducted in the presence of the prioress of St Teresa's Carmelite Convent. Also present at the meeting that afternoon was Father Luis Kondor, who was vice postulator of the cause of Blessed Francisco and Jacinta. Lucia was also asked whether it was true that the concerns she had were robbing her of her sleep and that she was praying night and day. She apparently responded, "It's not true. How would I be able to pray during the day if I did not sleep at night? How many things they attribute to me! How many things they make me do! They should read my book; the advice and appeals that correspond to Our Lady's wishes are there. **Prayer and penance, with great faith in God's power, will save the world.**"

On 9th November 1989, the Politburo finally decided to allow refugees to move across the border into West Germany including from East to West Berlin, and when this was reported in the news, thousands rushed to the 6 checkpoints in the city and as they passed through to the West they were greeted with flowers and champagne by jubilant West-Berliners. The Berlin Wall, that great symbol of communist oppression was completely torn down over the next two years.

- Chapter 9 -

Third secret made public

John Paul II made his second pilgrimage to Fatima from 10th to 13th May 1991 during which he again made an act of entrustment of the world to the Mother of God.

Then, on 28th June 1999, he promulgated the decree on the miraculous healing of Maria Emilia Santos, which finally cleared the path for the beatification of Francisco and Jacinta.

The pontiff later beatified the children in Fatima on 13th May 2000, which again was the anniversary of the first apparition, saying that they were two candles that God had lit to illuminate humanity in its dark and anxious hours. Lucia, who was ninety-three years of age at the time, was present at their beatification. Jacinta is the youngest non-martyred child to have been beatified in the Church.

It's quite incredible that even by this time the third secret of Fatima had still not been made public. However, John Paul II had now decided that the time was right for the revelations in Lucia's letter to be made known to the world. Prior to the release of the third secret, the pope wrote to Lucia on the 19th of April 2000 to say that he was sending Archbishop Tarcisio Bertone, the Secretary for the Doctrine of the Faith, as well as the Bishop of Leiria-Fatima to meet with her and to ask certain questions about the interpretation of the secret.

The meeting took place eight days later, on the **27th of April 2000** in the Carmel of Saint Teresa in Coimbra, where Lucia was handed the two envelopes. She first opened the white envelope and proceeded to read the letter inside, before confirming that it was her handwriting. Then the letter in Portuguese was read and translated by the Bishop of Leiria-Fatima, and Lucia said that she agreed with the translation.

She said that the vision of Fatima was above all concerned with the struggle of atheistic Communism against the Church and against Christians and that it described the terrible sufferings of the victims of faith in the twentieth century.

She was then asked, "Is the principal figure in the vision the Pope?" and she replied that it was, and Lucia also confirmed that all the children at Fatima had believed that the 'Bishop dressed in white' in the vision was indeed the Holy Father.

Lucia also said that she agreed with what John Paul II has said after the assassination attempt i.e. that '**it was a mother's hand that guided the bullet's path, enabling the Pope in his throes to halt at the threshold of death**.' The Pope had written this in his meditation from the Policlinico Gemelli to the Italian Bishops on the 13th of May 1994.

Archbishop Bertone asked Lucia why she had said that the letter could only be opened after 1960, and if it was Our Lady who had fixed that date. Lucia replied: "It was not Our Lady. I fixed the date because I had the intuition that before 1960 it would not be understood, but that only later would it be understood. Now it can be better understood. I wrote down what I saw; however it was not for me to interpret it, but for the Pope."

At the end of the meeting, Lucia was presented with a rosary from the Holy Father, and she in turn gave some of her hand-made rosaries to the ambassadors, to give to John Paul II. A few weeks later, on the 13th of May 2000, the pope was in Fatima for the beatification of Jacinta and Francisco. This was his third visit to Fatima, and at the end of the mass he took the opportunity to ask Cardinal Sodano to make a statement about the third secret, without revealing too much detail:

'Brothers and Sisters in the Lord! At the conclusion of this solemn celebration, I feel bound to offer our beloved Holy Father Pope John Paul II, on behalf of all present, heartfelt good wishes for his approaching 80th Birthday and to thank him for his vital pastoral ministry for the good of all God's Holy Church; we present the heartfelt wishes of the whole Church.

'On this solemn occasion of his visit to Fatima, His Holiness has directed me to make an announcement to you. As you know, the purpose of his visit to Fatima has been to beatify the two 'little shepherds.' Nevertheless he also wishes his pilgrimage to be a renewed gesture of gratitude to Our Lady for her protection during these years of his papacy. This protection seems also to be linked to the so-called third part of the 'secret' of Fatima.

'That text contains a prophetic vision similar to those found in Sacred Scripture, which do not describe photographically the details of future events, but synthesise and compress against a single background facts which extend through time in an unspecified succession and duration. As a result, the text must be interpreted in a symbolic key.

'The vision of Fatima concerns above all the war waged by atheistic systems against the Church and Christians, and it describes the immense suffering endured by the witnesses of the faith in the last century of the second millennium. It is an interminable Way of the Cross led by the Popes of the twentieth century.

'According to the interpretation of the 'little shepherds', which was also confirmed recently by Sister Lucia, 'the Bishop clothed in white' who prays for all the faithful, is the Pope. As he makes his way with great difficulty towards the Cross amid the corpses of those who were martyred (bishops, priests, men and women religious and many lay people), he too falls to the ground, apparently dead, under a hail of gunfire.

'After the assassination attempt of 13 May 1981, it appeared evident that it was 'a mother's hand that guided the bullet's path, enabling the Pope in his throes to halt at the threshold of death.' On the occasion of a visit to Rome by the then Bishop of Leiria-Fatima, the Pope decided to give him the bullet which had remained in the jeep after the assassination attempt, so that it might be kept in the shrine. By the Bishop's decision, the bullet was later set in the crown of the statue of Our Lady of Fatima.

'The successive events of 1989 led, both in the Soviet Union and in a number of countries of Eastern Europe, to the fall of the Communist regimes which promoted atheism. For this too His Holiness offers heartfelt thanks to the Most Holy Virgin. In other parts of the world, however, attacks against the Church and against Christians, with the burden of suffering they bring, tragically continue.

'Even if the events to which the third part of the 'secret' of Fatima refers now seem part of the past, Our Lady's call to conversion and penance, issued at the start of the twentieth century, remains timely and urgent today.

'The Lady of the message seems to read the signs of the times - the signs of our time - with special insight. The insistent invitation of Mary Most Holy to penance is nothing but the manifestation of her maternal concern for the fate of the human family, in need of conversion and forgiveness.'

'In order that the faithful may better receive the message of Our Lady of Fatima, the Pope has charged the Congregation for the Doctrine of the Faith with making public the third part of the 'secret', after the preparation of an appropriate commentary.

'Brothers and Sisters, let us thank Our Lady of Fatima for her protection. To her maternal intercession let us entrust the Church of the Third Millennium.'

On the **26th of June 2000**, about eighty-three years after Lucia had first been given the vision, the Vatican finally released the text of the third secret as contained in Lucia's letter, which is given below:

"I write in obedience to you, my God, who command me to do so through his Excellency the Bishop of Leiria and through your Most Holy Mother and mine.

After the two parts which I have already explained, at the left of Our Lady and a little above, we saw an Angel with a flaming sword in his left hand; flashing, it gave out flames that looked as though they would set the world on fire; but they died out in contact with the splendour that Our Lady radiated towards him from her right hand: pointing to the earth with his right hand, the Angel cried out in a loud voice: 'Penance, Penance, Penance!'

And we saw in an immense light that is God: something similar to how people appear in a mirror when they pass in front of it - a Bishop dressed in White - we had the impression that it was the Holy Father. Other Bishops, Priests, men and women Religious going up a steep mountain, at the top of which there was a big Cross of rough-hewn trunks as of a cork-tree with the bark; before reaching there the Holy Father passed through a big city half in ruins and half trembling with halting step, afflicted with pain and sorrow, he prayed for the souls of the corpses he met on his way; having reached the top of the mountain, on his knees at the foot of the big Cross he was killed by a group of soldiers who fired bullets and arrows at him, and in the same way there died one after another the other Bishops, Priests, men and women Religious, and various lay people of different ranks and positions.

Beneath the two arms of the Cross there were two Angels each with a crystal aspersorium in his hand, in which they gathered up the blood of the Martyrs and with it sprinkled the souls that were making their way to God."

Along with the text of the letter, a theological commentary on this vision was released by Cardinal Ratzinger, the Prefect of the Congregation for the Doctrine of the Faith. Cardinal Ratzinger would later become Pope Benedict XVI on the 19th of April 2005. His commentary read:

"A careful reading of the text of the so-called third 'secret' of Fatima, published here in its entirety long after the fact and by decision of the Holy Father, will probably prove disappointing or surprising after all the speculation it has stirred. No great mystery is revealed; nor is the future unveiled.

"We see the Church of the martyrs of the century which has just passed represented in a scene described in a language which is symbolic and not easy to decipher. Is this what the Mother of the Lord wished to communicate to Christianity and to humanity at a time of great difficulty and distress? Is it of any help to us at the beginning of the new millennium? Or are these only projections of the inner world of children, brought up in a climate of profound piety but shaken at the same time by the tempests which threatened their own time? How should we understand the vision? What are we to make of it?

"The first and second parts of the 'secret' of Fatima have already been so amply discussed in the relative literature that there is no need to deal with them again here. I would just like to recall briefly the most significant point. For one terrible moment, the children were given a vision of hell. They saw the fall of 'the souls of poor sinners'. And now they are told why they have been exposed to this moment: 'in order to save souls'- to show the way to salvation.

"The words of the First Letter of Peter come to mind: 'As the outcome of your faith you obtain the salvation of your souls' (1:9).

"To reach this goal, the way indicated - surprisingly for people from the Anglo-Saxon and German cultural world - is devotion to the Immaculate Heart of Mary. A brief comment may suffice to explain this. In biblical language, the 'heart' indicates the centre of human life, the point where reason, will, temperament and sensitivity converge, where the person finds his unity and his interior orientation. According to Matthew 5:8, the 'immaculate heart' is a heart which, with God's grace, has come to perfect interior unity and therefore 'sees God'.

"To be 'devoted' to the Immaculate Heart of Mary means therefore to embrace this attitude of heart, which makes the fiat – 'your will be done' - the defining centre of one's whole life. It might be objected that we should not place a human being between ourselves and Christ. But then we remember that Paul did not hesitate to say to his communities: 'imitate me' (1 Cor 4:16; Phil 3:17; 1 Th 1:6; 2 Th 3:7, 9). In the Apostle they could see concretely what it meant to follow Christ. But from whom might we better learn in every age than from the 'Mother of the Lord.'

"Thus we come finally to the third part of the 'secret' of Fatima which for the first time is being published in its entirety. As is clear from the documentation presented here, the interpretation offered by Cardinal Sodano in his statement of 13 May was first put personally to Sister Lucia. Sister Lucia responded by pointing out that she had received the vision but not its interpretation.

"The interpretation, she said, belonged not to the visionary but to the Church. After reading the text, however, she said that this interpretation corresponded to what she had experienced and that on her part she thought the interpretation correct. In what follows, therefore, we can only attempt to provide a deeper foundation for this interpretation, on the basis of the criteria already considered.

"'To save souls' has emerged as the key word of the first and second parts of the 'secret' and the key word of this third part is the threefold cry: 'Penance, Penance, Penance!' The beginning of the Gospel comes to mind: "Repent and believe the Good News" (Mk 1:15).

"To understand the signs of the times means to accept the urgency of penance - of conversion - of faith. This is the correct response to this moment of history, characterised by the grave perils outlined in the images that follow. Allow me to add here a personal recollection: in a conversation with me Sister Lucia said that it appeared ever more clearly to her that the purpose of all the apparitions was to help people to grow more and more in faith, hope and love - everything else was intended to lead to this.

"Let us now examine more closely the single images. The angel with the flaming sword on the left of the Mother of God recalls similar images in the Book of Revelation. This represents the threat of judgement which looms over the world. Today the prospect that the world might be reduced to ashes by a sea of fire no longer seems pure fantasy: man himself, with his inventions, has forged the flaming sword.

"The vision then shows the power which stands opposed to the force of destruction - the splendour of the Mother of God and, stemming from this in a certain way, the summons to penance.

"In this way, the importance of human freedom is underlined: the future is not in fact unchangeably set, and the image which the children saw is in no way a film preview of a future in which nothing can be changed. Indeed, the whole point of the vision is to bring freedom onto the scene and to steer freedom in a positive direction.

"The purpose of the vision is not to show a film of an irrevocably fixed future. Its meaning is exactly the opposite: it is meant to mobilise the forces of change in the right direction. Therefore we must totally discount fatalistic explanations of the 'secret', such as, for example, the claim that the would-be assassin of 13 May 1981 was merely an instrument of the divine plan guided by Providence and could not therefore have acted freely, or other similar ideas in circulation. Rather, the vision speaks of dangers and how we might be saved from them.

"The next phrases of the text show very clearly once again the symbolic character of the vision: God remains immeasurable, and is the light which surpasses every vision of ours. Human persons appear as in a mirror. We must always keep in mind the limits in the vision itself, which here are indicated visually. The future appears only 'in a mirror dimly' (1 Cor 13:12).

"Let us now consider the individual images which follow in the text of the 'secret'. The place of the action is described in three symbols: a steep mountain, a great city reduced to ruins and finally a large rough-hewn cross. The mountain and city symbolise the arena of human history: history as an arduous ascent to the summit, history as the arena of human creativity and social harmony, but at the same time a place of destruction, where man actually destroys the fruits of his own work.

"The city can be the place of communion and progress, but also of danger and the most extreme menace. On the mountain stands the cross - the goal and guide of history. The cross transforms destruction into salvation; it stands as a sign of history's misery but also as a promise for history.

"At this point human persons appear: the Bishop dressed in white ('we had the impression that it was the Holy Father'), other Bishops, priests, men and women Religious, and men and women of different ranks and social positions. The Pope seems to precede the others, trembling and suffering because of all the horrors around him. Not only do the houses of the city lie half in ruins, but he makes his way among the corpses of the dead.

"The Church's path is thus described as a Via Crucis, as a journey through a time of violence, destruction and persecution. The history of an entire century can be seen represented in this image. Just as the places of the earth are synthetically described in the two images of the mountain and the city, and are directed towards the cross, so too time is presented in a compressed way. In the vision we can recognise the last century as a century of martyrs, a century of suffering and persecution for the Church, a century of World Wars and the many local wars which filled the last fifty years and have inflicted unprecedented forms of cruelty.

"In the 'mirror' of this vision we see passing before us the witnesses of the faith decade by decade. Here it would be appropriate to mention a phrase from the letter which Sister Lucia wrote to the Holy Father on 12 May 1982: 'The third part of the 'secret' refers to Our Lady's words: 'If not, (Russia) will spread her errors throughout the world, causing wars and persecutions of the Church. The good will be martyred; the Holy Father will have much to suffer; various nations will be annihilated.'

"In the Via Crucis of an entire century, the figure of the Pope has a special role. In his arduous ascent of the mountain we can undoubtedly see a convergence of different Popes. Beginning from Pius X up to the present Pope, they all shared the sufferings of the century and strove to go forward through all the anguish along the path which leads to the Cross.

"In the vision, the Pope too is killed along with the martyrs. When, after the attempted assassination on 13 May 1981, the Holy Father had the text of the third part of the 'secret' brought to him, was it not inevitable that he should see in it his own fate? He had been very close to death, and he himself explained his survival in the following words: '... it was a mother's hand that guided the bullet's path and in his throes the Pope halted at the threshold of death." (13 May 1994)

"That here 'a mother's hand' had deflected the fateful bullet only shows once more that there is no immutable destiny, that faith and prayer are forces which can influence history and that in the end prayer is more powerful than bullets and faith more powerful than armies.

"The concluding part of the 'secret' uses images which Lucia may have seen in devotional books and which draw their inspiration from long-standing intuitions of faith. It is a consoling vision, which seeks to open a history of blood and tears to the healing power of God. Beneath the arms of the cross angels gather up the blood of the martyrs, and with it they give life to the souls making their way to God.

"Here, the blood of Christ and the blood of the martyrs are considered as one: the blood of the martyrs runs down from the arms of the cross. The martyrs die in communion with the Passion of Christ, and their death becomes one with his. For the sake of the body of Christ, they complete what is still lacking in his afflictions (Col 1:24). Their life has itself become a Eucharist, part of the mystery of the grain of wheat which in dying yields abundant fruit. The blood of the martyrs is the seed of Christians, said Tertullian. As from Christ's death, from his wounded side, the Church was born, so the death of the witnesses is fruitful for the future life of the Church.

"Therefore, the vision of the third part of the 'secret', so distressing at first, concludes with an image of hope: no suffering is in vain, and it is a suffering Church, a Church of martyrs, which becomes a sign-post for man in his search for God.

"The loving arms of God welcome not only those who suffer like Lazarus, who found great solace there and mysteriously represents Christ, who wished to become for us the poor Lazarus. There is something more: from the suffering of the witnesses there comes a purifying and renewing power, because their suffering is the actualisation of the suffering of Christ himself and a communication in the here and now of its saving effect.

"And so we come to the final question: What is the meaning of the 'secret' of Fatima as a whole (in its three parts)? What does it say to us? First of all we must affirm with Cardinal Sodano: '... the events to which the third part of the 'secret' of Fatima refers now seem part of the past'.

"Insofar as individual events are described, they belong to the past. Those who expected exciting apocalyptic revelations about the end of the world or the future course of history are bound to be disappointed. Fatima does not satisfy our curiosity in this way, just as Christian faith in general cannot be reduced to an object of mere curiosity. What remains was already evident when we began our reflections on the text of the 'secret': the exhortation to prayer as the path of 'salvation for souls' and, likewise the summons to penance and conversion.

"I would like finally to mention another key expression of the 'secret' which has become justly famous: 'my Immaculate Heart will triumph'. What does this mean? The Heart open to God, purified by contemplation of God, is stronger than guns and weapons of every kind. The fiat of Mary, the word of her heart, has changed the history of the world, because it brought the Saviour into the world - because, thanks to her Yes, God could become man in our world and remains so for all time.

"The Evil One has power in this world, as we see and experience continually; he has power because our freedom continually lets itself be led away from God. But since God himself took a human heart and has thus steered human freedom towards what is good, the freedom to choose evil no longer has the last word. From that time forth, the word that prevails is this: 'In the world you will have tribulation, but take heart; I have overcome the world' (Jn 16:33). The message of Fatima invites us to trust in this promise."

John Paul II had the original statue of Our Lady of Fatima brought to the Vatican on the 8th of October 2000 and he entrusted the new millennium to Mary in front of 1500 bishops from around the world.

Lucia passed away at the age of ninety-seven on Sunday the 13th of February 2005 in the company of the Carmelite sisters of her convent where she had lived for about 57 years, and the Bishop of Coimbra was also present with her when she died.

Pope Benedict XVI visited Fatima on the 12th and 13th of May 2010, and he said that 'he was bringing the problems and sufferings of the world to Fatima.' Benedict was also there to celebrate the 10th anniversary of the beatification of Jacinta and Francisco, and at the mass he celebrated he also marked the anniversary of the apparitions as well as the 1981 assassination attempt on John Paul II.

While he was at the shrine, he again affirmed that John Paul II firmly believed that the Virgin's unseen hand had rescued him from death in the assassination attempt. Benedict also said to Our Lady: "It is a profound consolation to know that you are crowned not only with the silver and gold of our joys and hopes but also with the 'bullet' of our anxieties and sufferings."

It's interesting that while he was on his way to Portugal, Pope Benedict XVI was asked if the suffering of John Paul II contained in Fatima's third secret could be extended to encompass the suffering of the Church with respect to the clerical abuse scandal. Benedict affirmed that it could, arguing that the Fatima message doesn't respond to a particular situation or time but that it offers a 'fundamental response' to the **constant need for penance and prayer**.

On 9th March 2013, a miraculous cure was attributed to Jacinta and Francisco Marto involving a five year old Brazilian boy named Lucas Batista Maeda de Mourao. On 3rd March, Lucas had fallen out of a window from a height of twenty feet, hitting the ground with his head and causing brain damage. In hospital, the boy's heart had stopped twice, and he was in a deep coma. The specialists said that the chance of Lucas surviving was low, and that if he did survive, then they would most likely have to deal with severe cognitive disabilities, or even the boy remaining in a vegetative state. His parents, Joao and Lucila, prayed to Our Lady of Fatima, and they also contacted the Carmelite Convent of Campo Mouro to ask the sisters to pray for their son. On hearing the request, one of the sisters ran to the relics of Francisco and Jacinta and prayed, "Shepherds, save this child, who is a child like you."

The family of Lucas, and the sisters from the convent continued to pray for the boy, and on 9th March he made a miraculous recovery. The doctors declared that the complete change in the boy's condition couldn't be explained scientifically, and the case was then passed on to the Congregation for the Causes of Saints in the Vatican to investigate.

Pope Francis mentioned the statue of Our Lady of Fatima in his very first Angelus prayer on Sunday the 17th of March 2013, and he also asked Cardinal Policarpo to consecrate his pontificate to Our Lady of Fatima. This was carried out on the 13th of May, which was the 96th anniversary of the first apparition. The Pope had the statue of Our Lady of Fatima brought to the Vatican on Saturday 12th October 2013, and he led a vigil that night in St Peter's square. Many in the crowd held their own replica statues as the statue from Fatima was carried through the square. The next day, Sunday the 13th of October, Pope Francis entrusted the world to Our Lady in front of a crowd of 100,000 people who had gathered in the square. This was the anniversary of the last apparition at Fatima.

In late February 2017, the Congregation for the Causes of Saints concluded that the healing of Lucas could not be scientifically explained, and so the canonisation of Jacinta and Francisco was now possible.

Another landmark was the completion of the diocesan phase of the beatification process for Sister Lucia on 13th February 2017. Her cause had begun on 30th April 2008, just three years after Lucia had died. It was a monumental task involving 30 people working full time, who had to meticulously analyse 10,000 letters and extensive diaries, as well as the statements given by 60 witnesses to her life. Normally there's a five year waiting period after a candidate's death before the diocesan phase can begin, but this condition was waived by the pontiff. In a similar way, Pope Benedict XVI had waived this condition in the case of the beatification process for Pope John Paul II.

Francisco and Jacinta Marto were canonised by Pope Francis at the Sanctuary of Our Lady of Fatima on 13th May 2017, the centennial of the first apparition. What is amazing is that it was Lucas Batista Maeda de Mourao who brought up the offertory gifts at the canonisation mass, and the pontiff embraced and kissed him lovingly at the altar.

Just two days later, all the bishops of Russia consecrated their country to the Virgin of Fatima, and a church is now to be built and dedicated there in her honour.

- Chapter 10 -
The message of Fatima

If we look at the words of Our Lady at the six apparitions, her message for mankind and for us as individuals is clear to see. At all six visits, Mary asked that the **rosary should be prayed** every day, and on three of them she went further and linked the praying of the rosary to peace in the world generally and specifically to the ending of World War I. At three of the apparitions, Our Lady said that **God is offended by sin**, and on another, that her Immaculate Heart was outraged by the sins of humanity.

On three occasions, she spoke of the need for **reparation** for the sins that had been committed by mankind, and on the second visit, Mary held a heart which was encircled by thorns. This indicates that we have a wider responsibility than just showing repentance for our own misdeeds and that as God's children we have a collective responsibility for the overall sinfulness present in the world. The altruistic act of offering up prayers in reparation for the sins of our fellow man is clearly pleasing to God, and the greatest example of a sacrifice being made for the sins of others is Jesus giving himself up for us at Calvary.

At three apparitions, Our Lady spoke about the **need for prayer**, and she said that sacrifices should be made for the **conversion of sinners**. She spoke of **Hell** and/or **Purgatory** on three of the visits and Our Lady gave a terrifying vision of Hell at the third apparition. At the fourth visit, she said that 'many souls go to Hell.'

Our Lady explained to the children at the second apparition, that Jesus wished to establish a devotion to her Immaculate Heart, and on the third visit, that God Himself wanted this to be done. On 13th June 1917, Our Lady gave the promise of salvation to all who made this First Five Saturdays devotion, and she also linked this, and the **consecration of Russia to her Immaculate Heart**, to peace in the world and to the salvation of souls.

At the third and fifth apparitions, Our Lady promised a miracle so that all would believe and this was the spectacular Miracle of the Sun on the 13th of October 1917 which was witnessed by tens of thousands of people.

On the third visit, Our Lady called for the consecration of Russia and she also gave the warning that if people did not cease offending God then a war worse that World War I would break out, and that 'a night illumined by an unknown light' would be the sign that the world was about to be chastised for its sins.

There are clearly two central themes here – the first is the need for **repentance** and the second is the need for **prayer**, and what's implicit in the words of Our Lady is that there are consequences for sin both at the level of the individual and at the macro level. So although Jesus has given himself up as a sacrifice for our sins, this clearly doesn't take away the ongoing necessity for us to repent.

There are also parallels here with the message that Our Lady gave to the 14 year old Bernadette Soubirous at Lourdes. At the 6th apparition in Lourdes on the 21st of February 1858, Bernadette could see that Our Lady looked sad and so she asked her, "What saddens you?"

Our Lady replied, "Pray for sinners."

Then at the 8th of the Lourdes apparitions on the 24th of February, Our Lady said: "Penance! Penance! Penance! Pray to God for sinners."

She repeated these same words at two subsequent visits on the 27th and 28th of February 1858.

It's clear from what Our Lady said at Fatima that God is offended and also outraged by the sins that are being committed in our world, but because God's love for His creation is so great and because He desires every soul to be saved and to enjoy eternal life with Him, He withholds the retribution that is warranted with immense patience. But ultimately there's a tipping point when the offences caused by sin necessitate divine intervention and justice.

Mary linked our sins to wars, famine, disease, and also to persecutions of the Church but she also offered us a remedy for this through repentance and prayer. Our Lady showed us clearly that the future of Mankind is not set in stone but that outcomes can be radically altered through our prayers and devotion, and an example of this is surely John Paul II surviving the attempt on his life which had been prophesied back in 1917. Our Lady herself is a remedy, if we would only embrace the devotion to Her Immaculate Heart that she asked for, and whatever prayers we make to Mary will be leveraged greatly to produce positive effects for us as individuals and for mankind.

Europe and other parts of the world witnessed a spectacular phenomenon when the night sky was illumined by an unknown light on the 25th of January 1938 and World War II soon followed. This terrible war was avoidable and was a direct consequence of mankind ignoring Mary's message and continuing to offend God through sin.

In the main, people ignored the call to repentance and they also failed to adopt the First Five Saturdays devotion that Our Lady asked for, and the Church was also very slow to heed the call to consecrate Russia to the Immaculate Heart of Mary, and our history books show us the terrible consequences of this inaction.

So is there a message from Fatima that is relevant for us today?

Firstly, we need to examine what motivated Our Lady to make the appearances that she did in 1917, and this was surely because our spiritual mother was so concerned about the large numbers of people that were in danger of going to Hell. She also came to warn mankind that the offences caused by sin would have a severely detrimental impact on our earthly lives too through wars, persecutions of the Church and disease.

She gave the horrifying vision of Hell to show that this is a reality and not a myth and to shake people from their complacency and to urge them to repent. Our Lady was therefore concerned with both our earthly life and with the eternal welfare of our souls.

She came to offer an effective remedy which would ensure ongoing peace in our world and which would secure our heavenly inheritance, and as Pope Benedict XVI said, the message of Fatima is that there is a **'constant need for penance and prayer.'**

The incredible promise that Mary gave to those who make the devotion of the First Five Saturdays cannot be taken lightly - Our Lady promised that she would assist at death with the graces necessary for their salvation. What more could we possibly ask for?

Unfortunately, man's spiritual path is currently diametrically opposed to what Our Lady called for at Fatima. We live in a time of great sinfulness, and yet this has coincided with an unprecedented decline in repentance, at least as measured by the number of people going to confession. The Centre for applied research on the Apostolate published a report in 2005 which showed that only 2% of Catholics attended confession regularly, and that three quarters never went at all.

People have never found the notion of having to repent easy to accept, even before the death and resurrection of Jesus. This is because it takes us out of our comfort zones and makes us admit that we have failings – failings which have compromised our relationship with God. But we should rather focus on the sanctifying grace that comes through the Sacrament of Confession, which removes all the guilt of sin and which draws us closer to God's love.

Unfortunately, there's a popular misconception that it's no longer necessary for us to repent because Jesus has already atoned for our sins anyway. But he himself said **after his resurrection** that we still need to confess our sins.

John 20:19: On the evening of that first day of the week, when the disciples were together, with the doors locked for fear of the Jews, Jesus came and stood among them and said, "Peace be with you!"

After he said this, he showed them his hands and side. The disciples were overjoyed when they saw the Lord. Again Jesus said, "Peace be with you! As the Father has sent me, I am sending you."

And with that he breathed on them and said, "Receive the Holy Spirit. If you forgive anyone his sins, they are forgiven; if you do not forgive them, they are not forgiven."

So it's clear that Jesus empowered his apostles to forgive sins, just as he'd done himself throughout his ministry. However, many Christians do not accept that this empowerment to forgive sins was passed on to the successors of the apostles and ultimately to priests in the Church. But this issue was addressed at the Council of Trent in 1551 AD where the following proclamation was made:

"The Lord instituted the Sacrament of Penance principally when after his resurrection he breathed upon his disciples and said: 'Receive the Holy Spirit. If you forgive the sins of any, they are forgiven; if you retain the sins of any, they are retained.' The universal consensus of the Fathers has always acknowledged that

by so sublime an action and such clear words the power of forgiving and retaining sins was given to the apostles and their lawful successors for reconciling the faithful who have fallen away after baptism."

The 'lawful successors' mentioned above are clearly ordained priests.

But just how far back in Church history can we trace the practice of confessing sins? Well, one of the proclamations of the 4th Lateran Council of 1215 AD was: "All the faithful should individually confess all their sins in a faithful manner to their own priest at least once a year."

But there's evidence that it was common practice for Christians to attend confession from long before this. For example in 459 AD, Pope Leo I wrote a letter to his bishops under the title, 'Magna Indignatione' in which he discussed confession. The pope wrote:

"With regard to penance, what is demanded of the faithful is clearly not that an acknowledgement of the nature of individual sins written in a little book be read publicly, since it suffices that the states of consciences be made known to the priests alone in secret confession."

Going even further back, we have a reference to confession in chapter 4 of the Didache, which is generally dated to the end of the first century AD. This brief treatise, also known as The Teaching of the Twelve Apostles, is the oldest written catechism ever found and it covers Christian ethics as well as Baptism and the Eucharist.

"In the church you shall acknowledge your transgressions, and you shall not come near for your prayer with an evil conscience."

But if we want evidence that repentance was actively encouraged by the apostles themselves after the resurrection, we just need to look at the book of Acts.

Acts 2:38: Peter replied, "Repent and be baptised, every one of you, in the name of Jesus Christ for the forgiveness of your sins. And you will receive the gift of the Holy Spirit.

Acts 3:19: Repent, then, and turn to God, so that your sins may be wiped out, that times of refreshing may come from the Lord, and

that he may send the Christ, who has been appointed for you –
even Jesus.

So it's clear that the practice of confessing one's sins goes right back to
the earliest beginnings of the Church. It's important for us to
remember that it's not the priests who are doing the forgiving, but that
they're acting 'in persona Christi' and that the grace of God's
forgiveness is just being channeled through them. This is why priests
use these specific words at confession: 'By the power given me by
Almighty God, I absolve you of your sins in the name of the Father
and of the Son and of the Holy Spirit.'

An example of the forgiveness that comes with repentance at the
macro level can be found in the biblical account of Nineveh. God was
angered by the sinfulness that was prevalent in this great city, and so he
sent the reluctant prophet Jonah to warn the people of its impending
destruction.

**Jonah 3:4: On the first day, Jonah started into the city. He
proclaimed: "Forty more days and Nineveh will be overturned."**

**The Ninevites believed God. They declared a fast, and all of
them, from the greatest to the least, put on sackcloth. When the
news reached the king of Nineveh, he rose from his throne, took
off his royal robes, covered himself with sackcloth and sat down
in the dust. Then he issued a proclamation in Nineveh:**

**"By the decree of the king and his nobles: Do not let any man or
beast, herd or flock, taste anything; do not let them eat or drink.
But let man and beast be covered with sackcloth. Let everyone
call urgently on God. Let them give up their evil ways and their
violence.**

**"Who knows? God may yet relent and with compassion turn from
his fierce anger so that we will not perish." When God saw what
they did and how they turned from their evil ways, he had
compassion and did not bring upon them the destruction he had
threatened."**

The lesson of Nineveh is that the punishment that's due for sin can be
put aside by God if we repent, and this was what Mary implored us to
do at Fatima in order to avert the chastisement of another war.

In the gospels, we read of John the Baptist calling people to repent through a ceremonial baptism in the River Jordan. John was the last of the Old Testament prophets and the first of the prophets of the New Testament, and he wanted people to repent in order to be in a fit spiritual state so that they could accept the teachings of Christ.

Matthew 3:1: 'In those days John the Baptist came preaching in the Desert of Judea and saying, "Repent, for the kingdom of heaven is near." This is he who was spoken of through the prophet Isaiah: "A voice of one calling in the desert, 'Prepare the way for the Lord, make straight paths for him.'"

John's clothes were made of camel's hair, and he had a leather belt around his waist. His food was locusts and wild honey. People went out to him from Jerusalem and all Judea and the whole region of the Jordan. Confessing their sins, they were baptised by him in the Jordan River.'

What's interesting is that Jesus himself made this baptism of repentance even though he was clearly without sin and he surely did this as an example for all of us to follow.

Matthew 3:13: Then Jesus came from Galilee to the Jordan to be baptised by John. But John tried to deter him, saying, "I need to be baptised by you, and do you come to me?"

Jesus replied, "Let it be so now; it is proper for us to do this to fulfill all righteousness."

Then John consented. As soon as Jesus was baptised, he went up out of the water. At that moment heaven was opened, and he saw the Spirit of God descending like a dove and lighting on him. And a voice from heaven said, "This is my Son, whom I love; with him I am well pleased."

It's fascinating that the voice of God was heard on this occasion, and it was the first of three situations when God was heard speaking. The other two occasions were at the transfiguration (Matthew 17:5), and also just after the triumphal entry of Jesus into Jerusalem just days before his death (John 12:28).

Jesus often spoke about the need for repentance during his public ministry, and an example of this was when he was asked what he thought about the execution of some Galilean men by the Roman Governor, Pontius Pilate.

Luke 13:1: Now there were some present at that time who told Jesus about the Galileans whose blood Pilate had mixed with their sacrifices. Jesus answered, "Do you think that these Galileans were worse sinners than all the other Galileans because they suffered this way? I tell you, no!

But unless you repent, you too will all perish. Or those eighteen who died when the tower in Siloam fell on them – do you think they were more guilty than all the others living in Jerusalem? I tell you, no! But unless you repent, you too will all perish."

In Matthew's Gospel, there's another example of Jesus warning the Pharisees about the need for them to repent.

Matthew 21:31: Jesus said to them, "I tell you the truth, the tax collectors and the prostitutes are entering the kingdom of God ahead of you. For John came to you to show you the way to righteousness, and you did not believe him, but the tax collectors and the prostitutes did. And even after you saw this, you did not repent and believe him."

At other times, Jesus described the joy that there is in heaven when a sinful person repents and turns away from sin, such as in the Parable of the Lost Coin.

Luke 15:8: "Or suppose a woman has ten silver coins and loses one. Does she not light a lamp, sweep the house and search carefully until she finds it? And when she finds it, she calls her friends and neighbours together and says, 'Rejoice with me; I have found my lost coin.' In the same way, I tell you, there is rejoicing in the presence of the angels of God over one sinner who repents."

The same theme is found in the Parable of the Prodigal Son, where the father looked out over the fields every day, hoping that his son would one day return to his love. When the young man finally came to his senses and asked for forgiveness, the father poured out his love upon him and fully restored him as his son.

A wonderful example of the compassion that Jesus will show us as individuals if we repent is found in Luke's Gospel, where a sinful woman put her shame and embarrassment aside to come to Jesus for forgiveness, without uttering a single word.

Luke 7:36: 'Now one of the Pharisees invited Jesus to have dinner with him, so he went to the Pharisee's house and reclined at the table. When a woman who had lived a sinful life in that town learned that Jesus was eating at the Pharisee's house, she brought an alabaster jar of perfume, and as she stood behind him at his feet weeping, she began to wet his feet with her tears. Then she wiped them with her hair, kissed them and poured perfume on them.

When the Pharisee who had invited him saw this, he said to himself, "If this man were a prophet, he would know who is touching him and what kind of woman she is, that she is a sinner."

Jesus answered him, "Simon, I have something to tell you."

"Tell me, teacher," he said.

"Two men owed money to a certain money-lender. One owed him five hundred denarii, and the other fifty. Neither of them had the money to pay him back, so he cancelled the debts of both. Now which of them will love him more?"

Simon replied, "I suppose the one who had the bigger debt cancelled."

"You have judged correctly," Jesus said.

Then he turned towards the woman and said to Simon, "Do you see this woman? I came to your house. You did not give me any water for my feet, but she wet my feet with her tears and wiped them with her hair. You did not give me a kiss, but this woman, from the time I entered, has not stopped kissing my feet. You did not put oil on my head, but she has poured perfume on my feet. Therefore, I tell you, her many sins have been forgiven, for she loved much. But he who has been forgiven little loves little."

Then Jesus said to her, "Your sins are forgiven."'

But perhaps we can take the greatest lesson on this subject from the final moments of Jesus' life as he hung on the cross at Calvary between the two thieves Dismas and Gestas.

Luke 23:39: One of the criminals who hung there hurled insults at him: "Aren't you the Christ? Save yourself and us!"

But the other criminal rebuked him. "Don't you fear God," he said, "since you are under the same sentence? We are punished justly, for we are getting what our deeds deserve. But this man has done nothing wrong."

Then he said, "Jesus, remember me when you come into your kingdom."

Jesus answered him, "I tell you the truth, today you will be with me in paradise."

So Dismas, the good thief repented at the very end of his life and made the perfect confession by acknowledging his sins and recognising the need for forgiveness, unlike Gestas. Dismas joined his sufferings to that of Jesus hanging on the cross right next to him and he was forgiven at that very moment, and this should give us all hope as it shows that it's never too late to repent and to turn to God.

But the response of Dismas and Gestas is also a lesson in how we should approach human suffering and terminal disease as the two men were experiencing exactly the same pain and yet their response to it could not have been more different. Gestas was full of anger, blaming and insulting Jesus and refusing to accept that he was going to die or that he had any need to ask for forgiveness and as a result he denied himself the joy of eternal life. Dismas, on the other hand, didn't allow his pain to make him bitter and angry with God, but rather he channeled his suffering into something positive by turning to Jesus.

At Lourdes in 1858, and again at Fatima in 1917, Our Blessed Mother made an urgent plea for us to repent and to turn to God in prayer, echoing what her son Jesus had said so often during his three year ministry.

- Chapter 11 -

Sins of our modern world

As God's laws are immutable they need to be the benchmark by which our actions are deemed to be sinful or not. It's easy to forget that God's definition of what constitutes sin is timeless, unlike man's laws which constantly evolve and redefine what actions are legal and which are not. Today there's a gulf between the two, and we now have protected in law actions which are clearly contrary to God's laws. Part of the reason why this has happened is the ascendency of individual liberty and a focus on protecting the rights of the individual.

But Jesus himself taught us that God's laws were permanent.

Matthew 5:17: 'Do not think that I have come to abolish the Law or the Prophets; I have not come to abolish them but to fulfill them. I tell you the truth, until heaven and earth disappear, not the smallest letter, not the least stroke of a pen, will by any means disappear from the Law until everything is accomplished.'

The Ten Commandments or Decalogue given to Moses on Mount Sinai were a simple and effective set of laws which everyone could understand regardless of their level of education, and by implementing them society would remain in an orderly state.

The second census of the Israelites wandering in the desert gave a population of 601,730 men over the age of twenty, and in addition to this there were 23,000 male Levites aged one month and older. So, if we were to include women and those under the age of twenty then we would surely have a figure of a few million Israelites at that time in history. To control this massive population that lacked the infrastructure and administration of a large city and that was often on the move, meant that a strict code of rules and observances had to be devised. So the Ten Commandments were an ideal core of rules to ensure stability and cohesion in this nomadic society of Israelites.

Subcategories to each commandment were inevitably added, and ultimately there evolved rules for worship, for separating diseased persons from the community, for minor and major offences against the person, etc. The phrase 'an eye for an eye and a tooth for a tooth' originated in this period and was the overarching principle of restitution or of seeking damages from someone who had caused you harm.

The commandments set forth that love for God must be above all else, and the first three commandments are centered on this theme – 'you shall have no other Gods before me', 'you shall not misuse the name of the Lord your God', and 'observe the Sabbath day by keeping it holy.'

They protect the family in the commandments 'honour your father and your mother', 'you shall not commit adultery' and 'you shall not steal' and they also protect marriage in the two commandments 'you shall not commit adultery' and 'you shall not covet your neighbour's wife.'

Finally the Decalogue protects the individual in the commandments 'you shall not murder', 'you shall not steal' and 'you shall not give false testimony' and this last commandment also helps to ensure integrity in the legal system.

Now if we judge our society against the Ten Commandments we see the perilous state of our world at this time. The first commandment is under threat through a tremendous rise in atheism in the world, and Jesus himself cited the most serious of all sins being blasphemy against the Holy Spirit.

Matthew 12:31: 'And so I tell you, every sin and blasphemy will be forgiven men, but the blasphemy against the Spirit will not be forgiven. Anyone who speaks a word against the Son of Man will be forgiven, but anyone who speaks against the Holy Spirit will not be forgiven, either in this age or in the age to come.'

Here Jesus is saying that there's no middle ground or grey area and that each individual has a choice to either reject Jesus or to accept him as the Messiah and a conscious decision to reject Jesus as God's son would deny that person access to the grace of salvation through his sacrifice on the cross. This passage also supports the teaching of the existence of Purgatory, as clearly some sins are able to be forgiven 'in the age to come.'

Luke 12:8: 'I tell you, whoever acknowledges me before men, the Son of Man will also acknowledge him before the angels of God. But he who disowns me before men will be disowned before the angels of God.'

John 3:16: 'For God so loved the world that he gave his one and only Son, that whoever believes in him shall not perish but have eternal life. For God did not send his Son into the world to condemn the world, but to save the world through him. Whoever believes in him is not condemned, but whoever does not believe stands condemned already because he has not believed in the name of God's one and only Son.'

Atheism is clearly a denial of God and in these texts Jesus reminds us that this is the only sin which can never be forgiven. In our modern western societies atheism is at an all time high, but there's also been a massive rise in the number of agnostics - people who say that they believe in God but who don't practice their faith, and an example of this is that only 13% of the UK population now attends church.

Then if we take the commandment 'you shall not kill', the most obvious contravention of this is abortion which is happening on an unprecedented scale in our society today. At the time of the apparitions at Fatima in 1917 abortion was illegal, and yet Our Lady was still greatly concerned about the level of sinfulness that was prevalent in the world, so how much more concerned must she be now?

Pope John Paul II released the encyclical '**Evangelium Vitae**' on the **25th of March 1995** concerning the inviolability of human life, and this specifically covered the acts of murder, abortion, and also euthanasia.

The number of abortions being carried out today is simply staggering, and the World Health Organisation estimated that for the period 2010 to 2014 there were 55.7 million abortions worldwide each year. The Guttmacher Institute estimated that the global annual rate of abortion for women of reproductive age (15 to 44 years) was 35 per 1,000 over this period. It's also estimated that over the period 2010 to 2014, 25% of all pregnancies ended in abortion worldwide, and that the figure for the United States was 17%.

In England and Wales alone in 2018 there were 205,295 abortions, and in the US there were about 1.21 million abortions each year for the period 2008 to 2011. These are abortions registered with the authorities, so the actual number will be far higher in these countries.

It's a sobering statistic that about 40% of premature babies born at 23 weeks in the UK now survive and yet the abortion limit is 24 weeks. In October 2019, new clinical guidelines were issued to doctors in the UK to say that they should routinely try to save the lives of babies born at just 22 weeks because survival rates had improved so much.

These are a few of the declarations that were made in the pope's encyclical of 25th March 1995:

Evangelium Vitae 58: 'Among all the crimes which can be committed against life, procured abortion has characteristics making it particularly serious and deplorable. The Second Vatican Council defines abortion, together with infanticide, as an 'unspeakable crime.''

Evangelium Vitae 61: 'The texts of Sacred Scripture never address the question of deliberate abortion and so do not directly and specifically condemn it. But they show such great respect for the human being in the mother's womb that they require as a logical consequence that God's commandment "You shall not kill" be extended to the unborn child as well….Christian Tradition - as the Declaration issued by the Congregation for the Doctrine of the Faith points out so well -- is clear and unanimous, from the beginning up to our own day, in describing abortion as a particularly grave moral disorder.'

Evangelium Vitae 62: 'Given such unanimity in the doctrinal and disciplinary tradition of the Church, Paul VI was able to declare that this tradition (regarding abortion) is unchanged and unchangeable. Therefore, by the authority which Christ conferred upon Peter and his Successors, in communion with the Bishops - who on various occasions have condemned abortion and who in the aforementioned consultation, albeit dispersed throughout the world, have shown unanimous agreement concerning this doctrine - I declare that direct abortion, that is, abortion willed as an end or as a means, always constitutes a grave moral disorder, since it is the deliberate killing of an innocent human being. This doctrine is based upon the natural law and upon the written Word of God, is transmitted by the Church's Tradition and taught by the ordinary and universal Magisterium.'

The Pope was correct in his comments in EV61 that direct abortion is not specifically covered in the Bible but it could be argued that it is covered by implication since the issue of the accidental harming or killing of an unborn child is specifically covered in **Exodus 21:22**:

'If men who are fighting hit a pregnant woman and she gives birth prematurely but there is no serious injury, the offender must be fined whatever the woman's husband demands and the court allows. But if there is serious injury, you are to take life for life, eye for eye, tooth for tooth, hand for hand, foot for foot, burn for burn, wound for wound, bruise for bruise.'

So it's clear from this text that the protection of the unborn child was actually enshrined in Mosaic Law.

This view was also echoed in the words of Tertullian in his work the Apologeticum, written around 197 AD. Chapter 9 verse 8:

"In our case, a murder being once for all forbidden, we may not destroy even the fetus in the womb, while as yet the human being derives blood from the other parts of the body for its sustenance. To hinder a birth is merely a speedier man-killing; nor does it matter whether you take away a life that is born, or destroy one that is coming to birth. That is a man which is going to be one; you have the fruit already in its seed."

The love that God has for innocent little children is also clear from Matthew's gospel.

Matthew 18:10: 'See that you do not look down on one of these little ones. For I tell you that their angels in heaven always see the face of my Father in heaven.'

Mary appeared at Fatima to warn us that our sins were greatly offending God and to reveal the consequences of this for us as individuals and at the global level. Mary warned us that the ramifications of inaction would be chastisement through disease, war, Russia spreading her errors throughout the world and persecution of the Church and the Holy Father, and all these facets of the warning came to pass. Arguably the greatest pandemic in history was Spanish Flu, and the carnage of World War II surely came about as a consequence of sin in our world, and over a period of 6 years 85 million people lost their lives. The Church was indeed persecuted during the period of Russian expansionism and an attempt was even made on the life of Pope John Paul II.

But the message of Fatima should not be seen as something that is rooted in history because it is surely just as relevant today as it was back in 1917, as we now face diseases like Covid-19 instead of Spanish Flu, and there is still the ever-present risk of war.

So it's clear that Mary called on mankind to repent and to pray, not just for ourselves and our personal failings, but to atone for the overall level of sinfulness prevalent in the world. We have a collective responsibility and this is evident in the 'Our Father' prayer where we say 'forgive us **our** trespasses' as opposed to my trespasses, and in the 'Hail Mary', where we say 'pray for **us** sinners'. Similarly, Our Lady's request for us to adopt the First Five Saturdays devotion is to make reparation for the blasphemies against her made by countless people throughout the world.

Some sins are clearly common to all ages but others have become far more prominent in our modern world such as atheism and abortion.

So in respect of sin, is the world in a better state now than it was in 1917?

Unfortunately, it would seem that it's a few orders of magnitude worse. Our Lady told the children in 1917 that God was offended and outraged by the sins being committed then, but how much more is He being offended today? Surely there has never been a greater need for repentance and for mankind to turn to God in prayer. In a radio message on the 26th of October 1946 to the U.S. National Catechetical Congress in Boston, Pope Pius XII said:

'The sin of the century is the loss of the sense of sin.'

These words were later quoted by John Paul II at the Synod of Bishops in October 1983, which was a month long synod convened to discuss 'Reconciliation and Penance in the Mission of the Church.' Here, John Paul II reiterated that penance was closely connected with reconciliation to God.

Regarding the vital role of Our Lady, John Paul II said the following:

'The first means of this salvific action is that of prayer. It is certain that the Blessed Virgin, mother of Christ and of the church, and the saints, who have now reached the end of their earthly journey and possess God's glory, sustain by their intercession their brethren who are on pilgrimage through the world, in the commitment to conversion, to faith, to getting up again after every fall, to acting in order to help the growth of communion and peace in the church and in the world.'

- Chapter 12 -

Purgatory

Our lady used the word 'Purgatory' at the first apparition on the 13th of May 1917, and so this chapter examines this state of existence that a soul experiences after death. It's interesting that the gospels record at least 28 references to Hell and 8 to Purgatory made by Jesus, although the references to Purgatory are implied as he didn't use that term. There are other references to Hell and Purgatory in the New Testament as well, such as in Paul and Peter's letters, and in the Book of Revelation.

The Catholic Church definition of Purgatory is that **'it is a place or condition of temporal punishment for those who, departing this life in God's grace, are, not entirely free from venial faults, or who have not fully paid the satisfaction due to their transgressions.'**

Church teaching on our personal (particular) judgment and on Purgatory is covered in the Catechism of the Catholic Church.

1022: 'Each man receives his eternal retribution in his immortal soul at the very moment of his death, in a particular judgment that refers his life to Christ: either entrance into the blessedness of heaven – through a purification, or immediately, - or immediate and everlasting damnation.'

1023: 'Those who die in God's grace and friendship and are perfectly purified live for ever with Christ. They are like God for ever, for they "see him as he is," face to face.'

1030: 'All who die in God's grace and friendship, but still imperfectly purified, are indeed assured of their eternal salvation; but after death they undergo purification, so as to achieve the holiness necessary to enter the joy of heaven.'

1031: 'The Church gives the name Purgatory to this final purification of the elect, which is entirely different from the punishment of the damned. The Church formulated her doctrine of faith on Purgatory especially at the Councils of Florence and Trent. The tradition of the Church, by reference to certain texts of Scripture, speaks of a cleansing fire.'

These pronouncements by the Church are informative, but it's also useful for us to look at the logic behind the existence of Purgatory, and at the biblical texts alluding to it.

God is of course perfect, and it's intuitive that evil could not exist in His presence, and this is also clear from Scripture.

Habakkuk 1:13: 'Your eyes are too pure to look on evil; you cannot tolerate wrong.'

This is also evident from the account of the Fall of Man in Genesis, where Adam and Eve had to leave the Garden of Eden because they had sinned.

Again we can conclude this from what God said to Moses on Mount Sinai before He came down on the mountain.

Exodus 19:12: "Put limits for the people around the mountain and tell them, 'Be careful that you do not go up the mountain or touch the foot of it. Whoever touches the mountain shall surely be put to death.'"

So it's logical that a soul would not immediately be able to exist in Heaven with Almighty God without undergoing purification.

It's clear from 2 Maccabees that it was customary to offer sacrifices for the souls of the dead as far back as the second century BC.

2 Maccabees 12:43-46: 'And making a gathering, he sent twelve thousand drachmas of silver to Jerusalem for sacrifice to be offered for the sins of the dead, thinking well and religiously concerning the resurrection (for if he had not hoped that they that were slain should rise again, it would have seemed superfluous and vain to pray for the dead). And because he considered that they who had fallen asleep with godliness, had great grace laid up for them. It is therefore a holy and wholesome thought to pray for the dead, that they may be loosed from sins.'

The Maccabees were the leaders of a Jewish rebellion against the Seleucid Dynasty, and books 1 and 2 outline some of their history from about 175 to 134 BC. The Seleucid Empire was a Hellenistic state formed under the rule of Seleucus after the break up of the empire that had been created by Alexander the Great.

Many of the Doctors of the Church covered the subject of Purgatory in their writings, such as Tertullian and Saint Thomas Aquinas. The first four Doctors of the Church from the West were the saints Ambrose, Augustine of Hippo, Jerome and Gregory the Great, and the first four from the East were the saints Athanasius, John Chrysostom, Basil the Great and Gregory of Nazianzus.

Today there are many more, such as Thomas Aquinas, who was given this title in 1568 by Pope Pius V, and others include the saints, Catherine of Siena, Teresa of Avila, and Therese of Lisieux.

Thomas Aquinas (1225-1274) was an Italian Dominican priest, and in his work, Summa Theologica, he wrote that souls in Purgatory suffer a twofold pain. The first is the delay of the Beatific Vision, and the second is the pain of sense, which is the fire of Purgatory.

He also wrote that in regard to both these pains, the least pain of Purgatory surpasses the greatest pain of this life. In terms of the pain due to the delay in experiencing the Beatific Vision, this was because 'the more a thing is desired, the more painful is its absence.'

Saint Augustine made a distinction between 'the temporal purifying fire of Purgatory that saves' and 'the eternal consuming fire for the unrepentant.' Thomas Aquinas also wrote that the souls in Purgatory are at peace, because they are assured of salvation, and that they are helped by the prayers of the faithful.

The doctrine on Purgatory was formally expressed in the Decree of Union drawn up by the Council of Florence in 1438, where the teaching on Purgatory was heavily debated. But what's surprising is just how far back the practice of offering prayers and the Eucharist for the souls of the dead is found in historical writings.

These practices are described by one of the early Church Fathers, **Tertullian**, who was the son of a centurion and who converted to Christianity in Carthage in 192 AD. His interest in the religion of Christianity came about because he was 'staggered by the constancy of Christians under brutal persecution.' It's thought that Tertullian worked for a time as an advocate in the law courts before taking to writing. Tertullian produced dozens of works including 'The Apologeticum' in which he described a report made by Pontius Pilate to the Emperor Tiberius that he had 'pronounced the unjust sentence of death against an innocent and divine person.' (Chapters 5 and 21).

Tertullian wrote in **De Anima: 'Full well the soul will know in Hades how to feel joy or sorrow even without the body. The 'prison' of the Gospel (Matt. v. 25) was Hades, and 'the uttermost farthing' the very smallest offence which had to be atoned there before the resurrection. Hence the soul must undergo in Hades some compensatory discipline without prejudice to the full accomplishment of the resurrection, when recompense would be paid to the flesh also.'**

Tertullian also described the practice of praying for the dead in chapter 3 of **De Corona militis**, which he wrote around 211 AD :

'We take also, in congregations before daybreak, and from the hand of none but the presidents, the sacrament of the Eucharist, which the Lord both commanded to be eaten at meal-times, and enjoined to be taken by all alike. As often as the anniversary comes round, we make offerings for the dead as birthday honours.'

In chapter X of his work **De Monogamia**, he wrote on the subject of the loss of a spouse and the importance of praying for the dead.

'Indeed, she prays for his soul, and requests refreshment for him meanwhile, and fellowship with him in the first resurrection; and she offers her sacrifice on the anniversaries of his falling asleep.'

So it's clear that it's been a long-standing practice both among the Jews and later the Christians to pray for the souls of the dead and inherent in this is the belief that souls after death can receive benefit from the prayers and the Eucharist offered up for them. From Maccabees we can see that the prayers and sacrifices were offered to free the souls from their sins, so that they could then participate in the resurrection.

Hell and Purgatory are subjects that priests seem reticent to tackle in their homilies today which is a great pity because failing to ever talk about the reality of these states leads the faithful into a false sense of security and breaks the link with the need for confession. Jesus spoke about Hell with alarming regularity and it's difficult to imagine that He would do anything else if he were on earth today.

It was during the Reformation that the reformers rejected the doctrine of Purgatory although it's interesting that there was hesitation by

Martin Luther. But let's look at the words of Jesus himself which may imply the purification of a soul after death.

Matthew 5:25: **'Settle matters quickly with your adversary who is taking you to court. Do it while you are still with him on the way, or he may hand you over to the judge, and the judge may hand you over to the officer, and you may be thrown into prison. I tell you the truth, you will not get out until you have paid the last cent.'**

Here we need to look at the context of this statement by Jesus. Viewed in isolation, this text seems to be covering litigation and damages but in verses 21 and 27 (i.e. before and after this statement) he spoke of the risk of sinners being sent to Hell and so it's clear that he wasn't talking about an earthly prison but a state of existence after death.

His words, 'you will not get out until you have paid the last cent' indicate that there is a debt of sin for which recompense must be made after we have died. Jesus was saying that we have an opportunity while we are still alive to put things right with God and so avoid the punishment due for those offences. Tertullian and Origen, as well as the saints Cyprian, Ambrose, and Jerome, all believed that the prison in this verse represented Purgatory, and that the last cent (or penny) represented the most minor sins that one commits in life.

We can confess our sins at any time to a priest and receive the grace of forgiveness, but we often hold back from doing this for a variety of reasons. It may be that we don't see the need to confess to a priest, asking ourselves why it's necessary to have a third party involved instead of just saying sorry to God directly. Or else we may believe that confession is now redundant because Christ's sacrifice at Calvary atones for all of our sins in any event.

However, we need to remember that Jesus empowered his apostles to forgive sins **after** his resurrection. If he believed that post-resurrection, it was no longer necessary for man to go through a priest to ask for forgiveness, then why did he empower them in this way after he had risen from the dead?

John 20:21: Again Jesus said, "Peace be with you! As the Father has sent me, I am sending you." And with that he breathed on them and said, "Receive the Holy Spirit. If you forgive anyone

his sins, they are forgiven; if you do not forgive them, they are not forgiven."

Another reason for putting off going to confession is pride, and another may be that we have rationalised away our failings and no longer really see them as sins anymore.

It's helpful for us to remember that in Confession and in the celebration of the Eucharist, the priest is acting 'In Persona Christi,' a Latin phrase meaning 'In the Person of Christ.'

Also, confession is a sacrament in its own right and so each time we attend we will receive the graces of the Holy Spirit.

Another reference to Purgatory is found in Mark's gospel.

Mark 9:49: **'And if your eye causes you to sin, pluck it out. It is better for you to enter the kingdom of God with one eye than to have two eyes and be thrown into hell, where 'their worm does not die, and the fire is not quenched.' Everyone will be salted with fire.'**

If we look at the first part of the reading (excluding 'Everyone will be salted with fire'), Jesus is talking about a permanent state which is Hell. The soul cannot be removed from this state because the condition of the soul is fixed at death and so Jesus was saying that we have the opportunity while we are alive to do something about our sinfulness.

In the statement, '**Everyone will be salted with fire**', Jesus seems to be referring to what we term Purgatory, a state where we are somehow sanctified before entering Heaven. Salt is added to food to improve it and to help bring out its flavour and so when Jesus says that everyone will be salted with fire, the objective of this 'salting' is clearly to improve us and not to harm us. We also need to remember that salt was a valuable commodity at the time of Jesus and the wages of Roman legionaries were partly paid in salt, hence the expression 'he's not worth his salt.'

In this reading, Jesus is saying that we should avoid sin at all costs because it could easily result in us forfeiting eternal life in Heaven. Perhaps part of the problem is that it's difficult for us to visualise the joy that awaits us in Heaven and to comprehend that our resurrected bodies will live on for all eternity. The human mind seems to struggle with non-finite concepts such as considering the enormous distances that stars are from the earth, or trying to imagine the sheer scale of the universe. This was perhaps why Jesus showed Peter, James and John the magnificence of the transfiguration at which they saw for a brief moment the transfigured Jesus radiant in glory with his face shining like the sun, and this is the same glory that awaits us at the resurrection.

1 Corinthians 15:42: 'So will it be with the resurrection of the dead. The body that is sown is perishable; it is raised imperishable; it is sown in dishonour, it is raised in glory; it is sown in weakness, it is raised in power; it is sown a natural body, it is raised a spiritual body.'

Philippians 3:20: 'But our citizenship is in heaven. And we eagerly await a Saviour from there, the Lord Jesus Christ. Who, by the power that enables him to bring everything under his control, will transform our lowly bodies so that they will be like his glorious body.'

The Church teaches that after death the soul leaves the body and we will then have our personal judgment by Jesus when our final state will be revealed. It's logical to assume that few people will have mastered all their weaknesses in this earthly life and so our souls would need to be brought to perfection in Purgatory before we could exist in God's presence. The nature of this purifying fire is unclear but it's reassuring to remember that souls experiencing this are in God's love.

Saint Catherine of Genoa (1447-1510) was given a vision of Purgatory which she described as a being a 'loving fire' and she wrote that the fire was to 'purge them of all the rust and stains of sin of which they have not rid themselves in this life.'

We don't talk much about '**the communion of saints**' anymore, but it's a teaching that we can help those in Purgatory by our prayers and by offering up masses for them, and conversely, the souls in Heaven can also help us on our earthly journey. Souls in Purgatory can no longer help themselves and they are reliant on the compassion of God, but also on our prayers, and this is why we should pray daily for the departed and why we should also encourage our children to do so.

The following are two readings from Matthew's gospel which also imply the existence of Purgatory, and that sins apart from blasphemy against the Holy Spirit can be forgiven in the afterlife ('the age to come.')

Matthew 11:11: 'I tell you the truth: Among those born of women there has not risen anyone greater than John the Baptist; yet he who is least in the kingdom of heaven is greater than he.'

If John the Baptist was the greatest man who had ever lived, and yet the least in Heaven was greater than John then it surely indicates that souls must be brought to a more perfect state after death.

Matthew 12:32: 'Anyone who speaks a word against the Son of Man will be forgiven, but anyone who speaks against the Holy Spirit will not be forgiven, either in this age or in the age to come.'

Saint Augustine, Gregory the Great, and the Venerable Bede are just some of the Doctors of the Church who took this verse as evidence of the existence of Purgatory.

Matthew 18:23: "Therefore the kingdom of heaven is like a king who wanted to settle accounts with his servants. As he began the settlement, a man who owed him ten thousand talents was brought to him. Since he was not able to pay, the master ordered that he and his wife and his children and all that he had be sold to repay the debt.

The servant fell on his knees before him. 'Be patient with me,' he begged, 'and I will pay back everything.' The servant's master took pity on him, cancelled the debt and let him go.

"But when that servant went out, he found one of his fellow servants who owed him a hundred denarii. He grabbed him and began to choke him. 'Pay back what you owe me!' he demanded.

"His fellow servant fell to his knees and begged him, 'Be patient with me, and I will pay you back.'

"But he refused. Instead, he went off and had the man thrown into prison until he could pay the debt. When the other servants saw what had happened, they were greatly distressed and went and told their master everything that had happened.

"Then the master called the servant in. 'You wicked servant,' he said, 'I cancelled all that debt of yours because you begged me

to. Shouldn't you have had mercy on your fellow servant just as I had on you?' In anger his master turned him over to the jailers to be tortured, until he should pay back all he owed. This is how my heavenly Father will treat each of you unless you forgive your brother from your heart."

Here, Jesus taught that our forgiveness will be determined by how forgiving we have been in our dealings with others and this dovetails nicely with the Our Father prayer where it states 'forgive us our trespasses as we forgive those who trespass against us.'

A talent was a unit of measurement and there were different brands of talent such as the Roman talent and the Babylonian talent, with a Roman talent weighing 32.3 kilograms. When a talent was used to measure metals it was usually for precious metals like silver and gold and the talent was formed as a massive ingot with a handle on top, and so a strong man could carry one in each hand for a very short distance.

In terms of its intrinsic value, a talent of silver would be worth the same as 32.3 kilograms of silver, and a talent was the equivalent of about 6,000 denarii. A denarius was a Roman silver coin roughly equivalent to a day's wages for a farm worker. A talent would therefore be about 6,000 days wages, or over 16 years work, bearing in mind that silver was far more valuable then than it is today.

So in the parable, the man owed the king a vast sum that was clearly impossible to repay in his lifetime, yet despite this the king cancelled this enormous debt as an act of mercy. In the same way, it's impossible for us to pay off the debt that's required in order for us to enter heaven by our own efforts. The glory of living in God's presence for eternity is incomprehensibly great, and we each have a debt of sin that we cannot possibly repay. However God writes off our debt through the sacrifice of Jesus at Calvary.

Instead of being grateful and showing mercy, the character in the parable pursues a poor man who owed him the equivalent of a hundred days wages, and then has him thrown into prison, and the response of the king was to turn him over to the jailers to be tortured.

Notice how Jesus doesn't say tortured forever but instead, 'until he should pay back all he owed' and so Purgatory unlike Hell is a transient state but our soul cannot leave there until it is sanctified.

There's also very strong support for Church teaching on Purgatory in two of Paul's letters.

1 Corinthians 3:11: 'But each one should be careful how he builds. For no one can lay any foundation other than the one already laid, which is Jesus Christ. If any man builds on this foundation using gold, silver, costly stones, wood, hay or straw, his work will be shown for what it is, because the Day will bring it to light. It will be revealed with fire, and the fire will test the quality of each man's work. If what he has built survives, he will receive his reward. If it is burned up, he will suffer loss; he himself will be saved, but only as one escaping through the flames.'

It's difficult to see how Paul could have been referring to anything other than Purgatory here, with the lighter materials such as wood, hay and straw being burnt away thus leaving what is precious behind. Our imperfections and attachments to sin will be burnt away in the spiritual fire of God's love, and as this fire is not permanent and does not destroy, we are able to escape through the flames. Saints such as Jerome, Augustine, Cyprian, Gregory the Great, and Ambrose, all believed that this text was a clear and obvious reference to Purgatory.

Hebrews 12:22: 'But you have come to Mount Zion, to the heavenly Jerusalem, the city of the living God. You have come to thousands upon thousands of angels in joyful assembly, to the church of the firstborn, whose names are written in heaven. You have come to God, the judge of all men, to the spirits of righteous men made perfect, to Jesus the mediator of a new covenant, and to the sprinkled blood that speaks a better word than the blood of Abel.'

The 'spirits of righteous men made perfect' clearly implies that after death our souls can be made perfect, and this purification comes from the grace of God's love, but again souls are also helped greatly by the prayers said for them and by masses offered up for their intention.

As mentioned at the beginning of this chapter, Our Lady used the word Purgatory at her first appearance on 13th May 1917 and so people who believe that the Church is in error in teaching the existence of Purgatory should ask themselves why she chose to use this particular term at Fatima.

- Chapter 13 -

Hell

On her third appearance at Fatima on the 13th of July 1917, Our Lady gave the children a terrifying vision of Hell, which Lucia described as follows:

'The rays of light seemed to penetrate the earth, and we saw, as it were a sea of fire. Plunged in this fire were demons and souls in human form, like transparent burning embers, all blackened or burnished bronze, floating about in the conflagration, now raised into the air by the flames that issued from within themselves together with great clouds of smoke, now falling back on every side like sparks in huge fires, without weight or equilibrium, amid shrieks and groans of pain and despair, which horrified us and made us tremble with fear. The demons could be distinguished by their terrifying and repellent likeness to frightful and unknown animals, black and transparent like burning coals.'

Terrified and as if to plead for succour, we looked up at Our Lady, who said to us, so kindly and so sadly:

"You have seen Hell where the souls of poor sinners go. To save them, God wishes to establish in the world devotion to my Immaculate Heart. If what I say to you is done, many souls will be saved and there will be peace…"

So Our Lady linked the devotion to her Immaculate Heart to the salvation of souls and also to peace in the wider world, and the apparitions at Fatima demonstrates the concern that our spiritual mother has for our welfare both in this life and the next.

During his three year public ministry Jesus was also at pains to warn us of the reality of Hell, and there are about 28 references to it in the gospels. This includes situations where Jesus alluded to Hell without naming it, by using phrases like 'weeping and gnashing of teeth', 'where their worm does not die', and 'where the fire does not go out' etc.

This eternal state of existence that Jesus warned us about is almost never mentioned in our modern world, and Hell now seems to have drifted into the realm of folklore and legend. However, the Church teaches that the soul of a person dying in a state of mortal sin would be unable to enter Heaven and would exist in the state we know as Hell for all eternity, and this is why it's so important for us to repent regularly, and the grace of Christ's forgiveness is always accessible in the confessional.

Clause 1035 of the Catechism of the Catholic Church states:

'The teaching of the Church affirms the existence of hell and its eternity. Immediately after death, the souls of those who die in a state of mortal sin descend into hell, where they suffer the punishments of hell, "eternal fire." The chief punishment of hell is eternal separation from God, in whom alone man can possess the life and happiness for which he was created and for which he longs.'

From the teachings of Jesus, we know that Hell is undoubtedly a place of suffering, that it is a place for souls who have died out of God's love, and that it is a permanent existence.

Matthew 5:21: "You have heard that it was said to the people long ago, 'Do not murder, and anyone who murders will be subject to judgment.'

"But I tell you that anyone who is angry with his brother will be subject to judgment. Again, anyone who says to his brother, 'Raca,' is answerable to the Sanhedrin. But anyone who says, 'You fool!' will be in danger of the fire of Hell.

"Therefore, if you are offering your gift at the altar and there remember that your brother has something against you, leave the gift there in front of the altar. First go and be reconciled to your brother; then come and offer your gift."

There's some controversy over the meaning of the word 'raca', as although it is present in the Greek manuscripts, it's not a Greek word. It's possibly referring to the Aramaic word 'reka' meaning empty one, empty-headed, or foolish. In Greek the word fool is translated as 'moros' which usually has a similar meaning to reka, but moros can also mean godless, which would be more insulting. Either way, it was definitely a word that was used as an insult.

So here Jesus is taking the commandments to another level, giving a quantum shift in their interpretation and showing that it is not just a contravention of the commandments that could result in us going to Hell, but that we could be sent there for sins which seem less significant to us.

Although Jesus went to great lengths to warn us of the existence of Hell, priests no longer seem to ever cover it in their homilies at all today perhaps out of fear of upsetting the congregation. After all, there's been a dramatic change in other areas of life in the last generation such as discipline in the home and in the school, where the pendulum has swung through 180 degrees. Priests may feel that the Church had placed too much emphasis on Hell and Purgatory in the past, hence the complete aversion to homilies on this subject today.

But does the Church have the right balance now? Perhaps we should ask ourselves, "If Jesus returned to Earth today would he be warning us about Hell or not?"

A frequently asked question is, "How could a loving God create a state like Hell?" But perhaps the premise of this question is wrong, and part of the answer can be found in **Revelation 12:7:**

'And war broke out in heaven: Michael and his angels fought with the dragon; and the dragon and his angels fought, but they did not prevail, nor was a place found for them in heaven any longer. So the great dragon was cast out, that serpent of old, called the Devil and Satan, who deceives the whole world; he was cast to the earth, and his angels were cast out with him.'

Revelation 12:3: 'And another sign appeared in heaven: behold, a great, fiery red dragon having seven heads and ten horns, and seven diadems on his heads. His tail drew a third of the stars of heaven and threw them to the earth.'

So this rebellion against God resulted in one third of the angels being banished from Heaven, and from then on there existed a state outside of Heaven that was under the control of Satan and his angels. Souls existing in this environment are clearly unprotected by God's love and will remain in a permanent state of separation from Him. This in effect is Hell - a state of permanent separation from the love of God.

So we shouldn't blame God for sending souls to Hell. Rather, an individual who chooses to reject God in his life, either by denying His existence or by living a sinful life and dying in an unrepentant state, has placed himself in this realm.

Matthew 5:27: You have heard that it was said, "Do not commit adultery." But I tell you that anyone who looks at a woman lustfully has already committed adultery with her in his heart. If your right eye causes you to sin, gouge it out and throw it away. It is better for you to lose one part of your body than for your whole body to be thrown into hell. And if your right hand causes you to sin, cut it off and throw it away. It is better for you to lose one part of your body than for your whole body to go into hell.

Here Jesus is asking us to go beyond the commandment 'Thou shall not commit adultery' and to go to the precursors of that sin. The sin of adultery doesn't just happen, and it begins long before the sexual act itself. Jesus is also showing that serious sin has an eternal consequence and that we must stop at nothing to protect our souls.

Mark 9:47: And if your eye causes you to sin, pluck it out. It is better for you to enter the kingdom of God with one eye than to have two eyes and be thrown into hell, where 'their worm does not die, and the fire is not quenched.'

This text also shows that a soul in Hell is there permanently, and this also links in with what Saint Paul wrote on the subject.

2 Thessalonians 1:8: 'He will punish those who do not know God and do not obey the gospel of our Lord Jesus. They will be punished with everlasting destruction and shut out from the presence of the Lord and from the majesty of his power.'

Jesus often mentioned fire when describing Hell and this was also evident in the vision that Our Lady gave to the children at Fatima, but many of the saints have had similar visions such as **Maria Faustina Kowalska** (1905-1938) who is regarded as one of the greatest mystics of the Catholic Church.

At the age of nineteen, she entered the Congregation of Our Blessed Lady of Mercy in Warsaw as Helena Kowalska and she was later given visions of both Purgatory and Hell. She described the fire in Hell as **'the fire that will penetrate the soul without destroying it - A terrible suffering since it is a purely spiritual fire, lit by God's anger.'**

Sister Faustina was also given a vision of Jesus in which he asked her to paint him just as he had appeared to her, and Jesus asked the mystic to put the words, 'Jesus, I trust in you!' at the bottom of the Divine Mercy painting. Our Lord also asked her to have the first Sunday after Easter designated the Feast of the Divine Mercy.

Jesus appeared to Sister Faustina again on the 13th of September 1935 while she was in Vilnius, and it was here that Jesus gave her the prayers which we know as the '**Chaplet of Divine Mercy.**'

Sister Faustina saw an apparition of an angel who was about to punish the world, but the words of the chaplet were then given to her and when she recited them she saw that the punishment that was about to afflict the earth was pushed away. The next day, Jesus appeared to her once more, and again gave the words of the chaplet and explained how they should be prayed.

The chaplet begins with one Our Father, one Hail Mary, and then the Apostle's creed. On the beads of the Our Father, one should say:

'**Eternal Father, I offer You the Body, Blood, Soul and Divinity of your dearly beloved Son, Our Lord Jesus Christ, in atonement for our sins and those of the whole world.**'

On the Hail Mary beads, one says '**For the sake of His sorrowful passion have mercy on us and on the whole world.**'

At the end of the five decades, Our Lord said that we should say three times: '**Holy God, Holy Mighty One, Holy Immortal One, have mercy on us and on the whole world.**'

During subsequent apparitions to Sister Faustina, Jesus gave the assurance that people who recited the chaplet would be given the grace of a happy and peaceful death, and he also said that people reciting the chaplet could ask God for everything that was concordant with His will. Jesus also urged people to recite this chaplet in the presence of those who were dying, and he said:

"**I desire to give inconceivable graces to souls who trust My mercy.**"

In 1936, Jesus again appeared to Sister Faustina when she was in Warsaw and it was then that he gave her the 'Hour of Mercy' prayer. This prayer is said at 3 o'clock each day, the time of the death of Jesus and the moment at which his sacrifice on the cross opened up a fountain of mercy for the world. He said that in this moment, mercy is opened broadly for every soul. The prayers are:

"You expired Jesus but the source of life gushed forth for souls and the ocean of Mercy opened up for the whole World. O Fount of Life, unfathomable Divine Mercy, envelop the whole World and empty Yourself out upon us.'

'O Blood and Water which gushed forth from the Heart of Jesus as a Fount of Mercy for us, I trust in You.'

Sister Faustina died of tuberculosis in her convent on the 5th of October 1938 at the age of just thirty-three. Fifty-four years later, on the 18th of April 1993, John Paul II beatified Sister Faustina and on the 30th of April 2000 she was canonised with the pope also declaring that the first Sunday after Easter would be the Feast of Divine Mercy.

The fire of Hell that Sister Faustina saw in her vision which in some ways resembles the appearance of physical fire but which doesn't combust material immersed in it, is reminiscent of what Moses witnessed with the burning bush.

Exodus 3:2: There the angel of the Lord appeared to him in flames of fire from within a bush. Moses saw that though the bush was on fire it did not burn up.

At Fatima, the children were deeply shocked by the vision of Hell and also surprised at the very large number of souls who were suffering there. Lucia recalled Jacinta sitting down on the ground and saying, "Oh Hell! Hell! How sorry I am for the souls who go to Hell! And the people down there, burning alive, like wood in the fire!"

She also wrote that on another occasion Jacinta had said, "Francisco! Francisco! Are you praying with me? We must pray very much, to save souls from Hell! So many go there! So many!"

Jacinta also asked Lucia why it was that all sinners weren't given a vision of Hell, saying, "Why doesn't Our Lady show Hell to sinners? If they saw it, they would not sin, so as to avoid going there! You must tell Our Lady to show Hell to all the people. You'll see how they will be converted."

In his gospel, Luke gives an account of Jesus being asked the question, "Are only a few people going to be saved?"

Luke 13:22: Someone asked him, "Lord, are only a few people going to be saved?"

He said to them, "Make every effort to enter through the narrow door, because many, I tell you, will try to enter and will not be able to. Once the owner of the house gets up and closes the door, you will stand outside knocking and pleading, 'Sir, open the door for us.' But he will answer, 'I don't know you or where you come from.'

"Then you will say, 'We ate and drank with you, and you taught in our streets.' But he will reply, 'I don't know you or where you come from. Away from me, all you evildoers!'"

And in Matthew's gospel there's also a passage where Jesus indicates that a large number of people will unfortunately go to Hell.

Matthew 7:13: "Enter through the narrow gate. For wide is the gate and broad is the road that leads to destruction, and many enter through it. But small is the gate and narrow the road that leads to life, and only a few find it."

There's been much debate about whether or not a narrow gate existed in the wall of Jerusalem named 'the eye of the needle' and it's possible that this was a small, inner gate and not one of the main gates of the city. The gate was apparently so narrow that traders would have to offload their goods and then lead the un-laden camel through the gate, and the analogy is that we need to let go of physical attachments before we can enter Heaven. Here, Jesus makes it clear that the easy path in life will lead to Hell but the narrow and difficult road in life is the one that leads to eternal life.

Matthew 10:28: 'Do not be afraid of those who kill the body but cannot kill the soul. Rather be afraid of the One who can destroy both body and soul in hell.'

Here Jesus explains that we need to see beyond the physical and to have in mind the protection of our souls which live for eternity and so our soul is by far our most precious asset. In this sense we must fear God, because although God is ever-loving, He is also a God of justice.

Another reference that Jesus made to Hell is found in **Matthew 13:47:**

"Once again, the kingdom of heaven is like a net that was let down into the lake and caught all kinds of fish. When it was full, the fishermen pulled it up on the shore. Then they sat down and collected the good fish in baskets, but threw the bad away. This is how it will be at the end of the age. The angels will come and separate the wicked from the righteous and throw them into the fiery furnace, where there will be weeping and gnashing of teeth. 'Have you understood all these things?'" Jesus asked.

Here, Jesus is using an analogy of catching fish which he knew that the uneducated people of the time could relate to, and the parable also explains the role that angels will perform at the end of time, and again Hell is described as being a fiery furnace. Jesus is at pains to get the message through because it's so fundamentally important, hence him asking them, "Have you understood all these things?"

But perhaps the most detailed description of Hell given by Jesus was in the Parable of the Rich Man and Lazarus.

Luke 16:19: "There was a rich man who was dressed in purple and fine linen and lived in luxury every day. At his gate was laid a beggar named Lazarus, covered with sores and longing to eat what fell from the rich man's table. Even the dogs came and licked his sores. The time came when the beggar died and the angels carried him to Abraham's side. The rich man also died and was buried.

"In hell, where he was in torment, he looked up and saw Abraham far away, with Lazarus by his side. So he called to him, 'Father Abraham, have pity on me and send Lazarus to dip the tip of his finger in water and cool my tongue, because I am in agony in this fire.'

"But Abraham replied, 'Son, remember that in your lifetime you received your good things, while Lazarus received bad things, but now he is comforted here and you are in agony. And besides all this, between us and you a great chasm has been fixed, so that those who want to go from here to you cannot, nor can anyone cross over from there to us.'

"He answered, 'Then I beg you, father, send Lazarus to my father's house, for I have five brothers. Let him warn them, so that they will not also come to this place of torment.'

"Abraham replied, 'They have Moses and the Prophets; let them listen to them.'

'No, father Abraham,' he said, 'but if someone from the dead goes to them, they will repent.'

"He said to him, 'If they do not listen to Moses and the Prophets, they will not be convinced even if someone rises from the dead.'"

It's implied that the rich man in this parable wasn't altogether bad because while he was suffering in Hell his thoughts were on trying to help other people, albeit members of his own family, and not just on himself.

And if we ask which commandment it was that he had broken that had condemned him to Hell, the answer is not straightforward either. Looking at a superficial level, we could argue that he had broken none of the commandments and conclude that he was purely guilty of being negligent of the suffering around him.

However, looking deeper we could argue that he had broken the commandment 'Thou shall not steal' in a more general sense by hoarding his wealth and thus maintaining a gross inequality in society. The rich man couldn't say that he was unaware of the man's plight, because he was right outside his gate and he would have seen him each time he entered and left the house. Indeed he even knew the beggar's name was Lazarus.

It's also easy for us to be negligent of the poor around us and to walk past a modern-day Lazarus who's in dire need of help, and it's sobering to think that every beggar we see was once a young child in a school photograph. There was potential there, as there was in all the other children in the photo, but circumstances, probably including making poor choices in life, resulted in the person being where they are now.

The rich man passed Lazarus every day and probably avoided eye contact with him, as we may sometimes do ourselves when passing a beggar sitting on the ground with his blanket, his tin can and his dog. And so it would appear from this parable that we can be sent to Hell for more subtle reasons than the overt breaking of commandments.

In the case of the rich man, his sin was that he'd ignored the plight of those suffering around him when he was undoubtedly in a position to help, and this complements the Parable of the Good Samaritan which Jesus taught in response to the question 'Who is my neighbour?'

In the parable, Hell is again described as a place of agony and it's interesting that those in Hell were somehow aware of the joys of those in Heaven. After death, the rich man had become fully aware of the need for repentance but it was too late as he'd been judged and his state was then fixed for all eternity. The rich man focused on his family, realising that unless they repented then they would also share the same fate and so he asked Abraham to 'send' Lazarus to his father's house.

But the tone of this indicates another problem that the rich man had, as despite him being in Hell, he still viewed Lazarus as somehow inferior, seeing him as a servant to be bossed around. The great chasm that Jesus described is interesting and it shows that it's impossible for a soul to ever move from the one state to the other.

In another of his parables, Jesus reminds us that we need to be prepared at all times because we don't know when we'll be called from this life.

Matthew 25:1: "At that time the kingdom of heaven will be like ten virgins who took their lamps and went out to meet the bridegroom. Five of them were foolish and five were wise. The foolish ones took their lamps but did not take any oil with them. The wise ones, however, took oil in jars along with their lamps.**

"The bridegroom was a long time in coming, and they all became drowsy and fell asleep. At midnight the cry rang out: 'Here's the bridegroom! Come out to meet him!' Then all the virgins woke up and trimmed their lamps.

"The foolish ones said to the wise, 'Give us some of your oil; our lamps are going out.' 'No,' they replied, 'there may not be enough for both us and you. Instead, go to those who sell oil and buy some for yourselves.'

"But while they were on their way to buy the oil, the bridegroom arrived. The virgins who were ready went in with him to the wedding banquet. And the door was shut. Later the others also

came. 'Lord, Lord,' they said, 'open the door for us!' But he replied, 'Truly I tell you, I don't know you.' Therefore keep watch, because you do not know the day or the hour."

Here Jesus is saying that we need to live our lives in a state of grace, prepared at any time to be called to give an account of ourselves. After all, it's easy for us to get so caught up in the material things of life that we forget the importance of developing our relationship with God.

The parable also reminds us that we need to think through what's required of us as Christians and this has parallels with the stories Jesus told of the man who intended to build a tower, and of the king with 10,000 men who intended to fight another king with 20,000 men. Jesus said that surely they would have to think through what was required in advance.

What's disconcerting about this parable is that the five virgins were not deemed fit for Heaven even though they'd done many things right. In the same way, the rich ruler who approached Jesus and asked him what he had to do to inherit eternal life had never broken a single commandment and yet he was considered unworthy (Matthew 19:16).

Further on in Matthew's gospel, Jesus again illustrates how being negligent of the poor in our midst can result in our condemnation.

Matthew 25:41: "**Then he will say to those on his left, 'Depart from me, you who are cursed, into the eternal fire prepared for the devil and his angels. For I was hungry and you gave me nothing to eat, I was thirsty and you gave me nothing to drink, I was a stranger and you did not invite me in, I needed clothes and you did not clothe me, I was sick and in prison and you did not look after me.'**

"They also will answer, 'Lord, when did we see you hungry or thirsty or a stranger or needing clothes or sick or in prison, and did not help you?'

"He will reply, 'Truly I tell you, whatever you did not do for one of the least of these, you did not do for me.' Then they will go away to eternal punishment, but the righteous to eternal life."

This text, like the Parable of the Good Samaritan, reveals the simple, practical ways in which Jesus expects us as Christians to treat our neighbour, and regarding the welcoming of strangers it's good to remind ourselves that the Holy Family also once lived as refugees in a foreign land when they had to flee to Egypt to escape the brutality of King Herod.

God is abundant in compassion and love, and showing love to the sick and to the needy has always been part of God's plan for Mankind.

Deuteronomy 10:18: 'He defends the cause of the fatherless and the widow, and loves the alien (stranger), giving him food and clothing. And you are to love those who are aliens, for you yourselves were aliens in Egypt.'

So at Fatima in 1917, Our Lady gave the children a terrifying vision of Hell. Mary did this to show us the reality of this permanent state of separation from God's love, and it was done out of concern for us by Our Blessed Mother.

Mary also reminded us to pray the rosary, and she gave us the First Five Saturdays devotion to help us as individuals but also to help save other souls from going to Hell.

- Chapter 14 -

The Immaculate Conception

This chapter looks at the unique qualities of Mary that made it possible for her to carry Jesus in her womb and also at her ongoing role in drawing us to the love of God. The word 'immaculate' was used by Mary herself at the apparitions at both Lourdes and Fatima.

It's surely no coincidence that Mary chose to appear at Lourdes so soon after the doctrine of the Immaculate Conception had been declared an infallible teaching of the Church by Pope Pius IX in 1854.

It's also remarkable that Mary revealed to Bernadette that she was the Immaculate Conception on 25th March 1858 which of all the days in the Church calendar is the Feast Day of The Annunciation. This was when the Angel Gabriel announced to Mary that she would conceive through the power of the Holy Spirit and carry the Son of God in her womb, and so this declaration by Our Lady at Lourdes can logically be seen as her endorsement of this teaching of the Church.

Understanding the significance of the Immaculate Conception is necessary for us to understand the unique position that Mary holds of all human beings and to see how she's an intrinsic part of God's plan.

Pope Pius IX defined this teaching in 1854, when he wrote:

"We declare, pronounce and define that the doctrine which holds that the Blessed Virgin Mary, at the first instant of her conception, by a singular privilege and grace of the Omnipotent God, in virtue of the merits of Jesus Christ, the Saviour of mankind, was preserved immaculate from all stain of original sin, has been revealed by God, and therefore should firmly and constantly be believed by all the faithful."

According to both Christian and Islamic tradition, the mother of the Virgin Mary was Anne and she's mentioned in the apocryphal Gospel of James which was written in Greek around 150 AD and the text also mentions Anne's husband, Joachim of Nazareth.

Another teaching of the Church is the **Perpetual Virginity of Mary** and here there's been some contention about the mention in the Gospels of Jesus having had brothers but this is simply down to etymology. The Old Testament was written in Hebrew and in this language there's no word equivalent to the English words for cousin or nephew and so they're all described as being brothers.

Now the Greek word for brother is 'adelphos' which is a union of 'a' for same and 'delph' for womb, so when the Old Testament writings were translated into Greek the translators used the word 'adelphos' to describe brother, but this word was also used to describe a cousin or a nephew. Later, the authors of the New Testament, who wrote mainly in Greek from outset, continued to use the word adelphos in this way and so the brothers mentioned were not sons of Mary, but rather other relatives of Jesus, and as Saint Jerome taught in the 5th century they were most probably his cousins.

The question could be asked why it was necessary for the mother of the Messiah to be completely devoid of sin, and to answer this we only need to look at the history of the Israelites wandering in the desert as this shows us that nothing imperfect can exist with God. We know this because when God was present on Mount Sinai He warned Moses not to allow anyone to come anywhere near His presence.

Exodus 19:12: Put limits for the people around the mountain and tell them, 'Be careful that you do not go up the mountain or touch the foot of it. Whoever touches the mountain shall surely be put to death.'

Exodus 33:19: "I will have mercy on whom I will have mercy, and I will have compassion on whom I will have compassion." "But," he said, "You cannot see my face, for no one may see me and live."

Another way of viewing this is to say that it's physically impossible for God to be in the presence of anything which is imperfect, and an analogy might be when you take two very powerful magnets and try to push the ends of the magnets with the same polarity together. It just cannot happen as the magnets simply repel each other.

Yet despite God being perfect and man being inherently sinful, He still wanted to unite Himself with His creation in the most intimate and loving way possible, which was by allowing His divine Son Jesus to become man. This shows the depth of love that God has for us in that He was prepared to allow Jesus to assume the lowly condition of a human being with all the vulnerability inherent in the human state, and so Jesus would experience the full range of emotions, dangers and temptations that we all do in our day-to-day lives.

However, although Jesus became man, he would always retain his divinity, and appreciating this is essential to our understanding of why Mary had to be immaculate. Mary being devoid of sin was the only environment in which the mutually exclusive entities of a perfect God and man could co-exist. Quite simply the conception of Jesus would have been impossible if it were not for this unique quality of Mary.

Matthew's gospel mentions an angel appearing to Joseph in a dream after he'd discovered that Mary was pregnant, and the angel explained to him that what had been conceived in Mary's womb was through divine intervention.

Matthew 1:20: But after he had considered this, an angel of the Lord appeared to him in a dream and said, "Joseph, son of David, do not be afraid to take Mary home as your wife, because what is conceived in her is from the Holy Spirit. She will give birth to a son, and you are to give him the name Jesus, because he will save his people from their sins."

Now in Luke's gospel we read of the appearance of the Angel Gabriel to Mary in Nazareth, and of the conversation that they had.

Luke 1:26: In the sixth month, God sent the angel Gabriel to Nazareth, a town in Galilee, to a virgin pledged to be married to a man named Joseph, a descendent of David. The virgin's name was Mary. The angel went to her and said, "Greetings, you who are highly favoured! The Lord is with you."

Mary was greatly troubled at his words and wondered what kind of greeting this might be. But the angel said to her, "Do not be afraid, Mary, you have found favour with God. You will be with child and give birth to a son, and you are to give him the name Jesus. He will be great and will be called the Son of the Most High. The Lord God will give him the throne of his father David, and he will reign over the house of Jacob for ever; his kingdom will never end."

"How will this be" Mary asked the angel, "since I am a virgin?"

The angel answered, "The Holy Spirit will come upon you and the power of the Most High will over-shadow you. So the holy one to be born will be called the Son of God. Even Elizabeth your relative is going to have a child in her old age, and she who was said to be barren is in her sixth month. For nothing is impossible with God."

"I am the Lord's servant," Mary answered. "May it be to me as you have said." Then the angel left her.

At that time Mary got ready and hurried to a town in the hill country of Judea, where she entered Zechariah's home and greeted Elizabeth. When Elizabeth heard Mary's greeting, the baby leaped in her womb, and Elizabeth was filled with the Holy Spirit. In a loud voice she exclaimed, "Blessed are you among women, and blessed is the child you will bear!"

Although uncertain, it's generally thought that Elizabeth and Zechariah lived in the town of Ein Karem which was about 6 kilometres west of Jerusalem, and it would have taken Mary several days to have made the 145 kilometre journey there from Nazareth. So between the greeting of the Angel Gabriel, and the exclamation of Elizabeth we have the first part of the 'Hail Mary' prayer. The Hail Mary is of course recited in the praying of the rosary, which the Virgin Mary and Bernadette often prayed in unison during the Lourdes apparitions.

It's remarkable that the Son of God being born to a virgin was actually prophesied seven hundred years earlier by Isaiah, as was the prophecy of Micah that the Messiah would be born in the insignificant village of Bethlehem which only had a population of several hundred people.

Isaiah 7:13: Then Isaiah said, "Hear now, you house of David! Is it not enough to try the patience of men? Will you try the patience of my God also? Therefore the Lord himself will give you a sign: The virgin will be with child and will give birth to a son, and will call him Immanuel" (meaning God with us).

As Isaiah said, this sign for mankind would not be given by a prophet but by God Himself, and so we can see here the unique position that Mary occupies of all the women who have ever lived - she was completely without sin and therefore able to carry the Christ in her womb.

Mary accepted the plan that God had for her and all of the trials associated with it without any hesitation. She submitted wholly to the will of God just as Bernadette did at Lourdes and in the same trusting way that Lucia, Francisco and Jacinta did at Fatima.

Mary stood at the cross at Calvary as her son suffered, and her whole life shows us the selfless love and dedication that she had as a mother. It's self-evident that she knows Jesus better than anyone could ever do and she also knows how to bring a soul to her son's love and to the joy of everlasting life in heaven if we will only allow her to do so.

Mary had a difficult life starting from before she even gave birth to Jesus, having to travel all the way from Nazareth to Bethlehem in order to comply with the decree of Caesar Augustus that a population census be taken of the Roman Empire. The population of male Roman citizens would have exceeded 5 million at this time in history because the later census conducted by Claudius in 48 AD gave a total of 5,984,072 men.

When Jesus was eight days old, Mary and Joseph took him to the temple to be circumcised and they were met in the temple courts by a devout Jew named Simeon who had been assured by God that he wouldn't die until he'd seen the Christ.

Luke 2:34: Then Simeon blessed them and said to Mary, his mother: "This child is destined to cause the falling and rising of many in Israel, and to be a sign that will be spoken against, so that the thoughts of many hearts will be revealed. And a sword will pierce your own soul too."

Simeon's caution that a sword would pierce her soul was one of the seven dolours, or sorrows, that Mary would face, and she would have to worry about the meaning of Simeon's words all her life. Another sorrow was when the Holy family had to flee from the tyrant, Herod the Great and live in Egypt for a few years, far away from their families and loved ones. The third sorrow was when Jesus went missing for four days until his distraught parents found him sitting in the temple with the teachers of the Law.

The fourth sorrow was when Mary met her beloved son on his way to Calvary lacerated from the scourging and struggling to stay on his feet, and the fifth was when Our Lady stood near the foot of the cross at

Golgotha and watched her son die. Mary's sixth sorrow was to see the centurion Longinus pierce the side of Jesus with a lance, and shortly after this, receiving the body of her son into her arms. The last sorrow was to see the body of Jesus being placed in the nearby tomb by Nicodemus and Joseph of Arimathea. These two men were both members of the 69 strong Great Sanhedrin of Jerusalem which had earlier sanctioned the arrest of Jesus, but they were also secret followers of his.

John, the disciple whom Jesus loved, was the only apostle actually present at the crucifixion and it was as he was hanging in agony on the cross that Jesus gave this disciple into the care of his mother Mary.

John 19:25: Near the cross of Jesus stood his mother, his mother's sister, Mary the wife of Clopas, and Mary Magdalene. When Jesus saw his mother there, and the disciple whom he loved standing near by, he said to his mother, "Dear woman, here is your son." And to the disciple, "Here is your mother." From that time on, this disciple took her into his home.

The depth of love between mother and son was plain to see at Calvary and the fact that Jesus entrusted Mary to John shows his great concern for her wellbeing. But Jesus surely didn't only give John a spiritual mother in Mary but he also made Mary our mother and indeed the mother of all of God's children. Entrusting John into Mary's care also shows that Jesus intended for Mary to be involved in the growth of the fledgling Church going forward, and we can see her involvement in **Acts1:14: 'They all joined together constantly in prayer, along with the women and Mary the mother of Jesus, and with his brothers.'**

Jesus knew the vital role that John would later play as an evangelist, as the author of the last of the gospels and at least part of the Book of Revelation. There was mutual benefit to be derived from Mary helping John and vice versa, and they would both need each other's support over the rest of their lives. No-one knew Jesus quite like Mary, and we can only speculate about how often John must have consulted Mary before putting quill to parchment, and we'll also never know the wealth of knowledge that Jesus shared with his mother during the thirty years that he lived at home before the start of his public ministry.

Reading the account of the Wedding at Cana, it's clear that Mary already knew that Jesus could work miracles and it makes one wonder if he'd performed some miracles before his public ministry had even begun.

There are two traditions in the Church regarding where Mary was assumed into Heaven, with one tradition holding that this was in Jerusalem but the other placing the event at Ephesus, and it's generally accepted that the apostle John died at Selcuk, which is about 3 kilometres from Ephesus in modern day Turkey.

The tradition that Mary lived in Ephesus was first proposed by Epiphanius, who was the Bishop of Salamis in Cyprus in the fourth century but the Eastern Orthodox Church also holds that Mary lived in the vicinity of this city. Proponents of the Ephesus tradition believe that Mary lived on the slopes of the Bulbul Mountain at a site called Meryemana, The Virgin Mary's house, and although the original building is long gone, another was rebuilt on the site and has been preserved to this day. Interestingly, there's a spring in the garden which many believe has been a source of healing and mass is held outdoors there in the evenings.

During his brutal persecution of Christians, the Emperor Domitian attempted to kill John by having him poisoned and then thrown into a huge cauldron of boiling oil in front of a packed Colosseum in Rome. The execution attempts failed and he miraculously emerged unhurt from the boiling oil which apparently resulted in a very large number of conversions to Christianity, but Domitian then exiled him to the penal island of Patmos. This event was described by the ancient historian, Tertullian in his work, 'The prescription against heretics.'

'How happy is its church, on which apostles poured forth all their doctrine along with their blood! Where Peter endures a passion like his Lord's! Where Paul wins his crown in a death like John's, where the Apostle John was first plunged, unhurt, into boiling oil, and thence remitted to his island-exile!' (Chapter 36, The Prescription against Heretics)

Domitian ruled for fifteen years, the longest of any emperor since Tiberius, but he was finally assassinated by officials of the court on 18th September 96 AD. During his authoritarian rule Domitian had severely restricted the powers of the Senate thus creating great animosity, and he was portrayed as being a cruel and paranoid tyrant by the ancient historians Tacitus, Suetonius and also Pliny the Younger.

After the death of Domitian, John was finally able to return to Ephesus, which was about a year after his exile, and his was the last of the gospels to be written, and in John's final years he taught Polycarp, who later become the bishop of Smyrna. John is thought to have died around 100 AD when he was about 94 years of age.

The Catholic Church has never formally pronounced on whether Mary died or not but has always taught that she was assumed into heaven, both body and soul. At the Council of Chalcedon in 451 AD, the Emperor Marcian asked the Patriarch of Jerusalem to bring the relics of Mary through to Constantinople so that they could be enshrined there, but the Patriarch reported back that there were no relics of Mary in Jerusalem. He said that Mary had died in the presence of the apostles, but that her tomb when opened later was found to be empty and so the apostles concluded that her body had been taken up into heaven.

The Church of the Sepulchre of Saint Mary at the foot of the Mount of Olives has a crypt which many believe was the resting place of Mary until her assumption and that it was this tomb that when opened was found to be empty. Over the centuries, various churches have been built and later destroyed on this site, but the crypt has always been left undamaged. Even in 1187, when Saladin destroyed the church that had been built by the Crusaders in 1130, he didn't damage the crypt itself.

The actual site of where Mary is thought by many to have died (as opposed to where she may have been buried) also became a place of pilgrimage. The Benedictine Abbey of the Dormition of Mary stands on this site today and is located on Mount Zion just outside the old city walls near the Zion gate.

If we will only permit it, Mary will act as a powerful intercessor between us and her son, Jesus. While Jesus was alive on earth, he listened to Mary, as is evident from the account of the Miracle at Cana where Jesus converted between 450 and 690 litres of water into wine. It's clear from John's account that the initial reaction of Jesus was not to get involved in working this miracle at all but that he was motivated to do so by the plea of his mother. In the same way, we can have full confidence that Mary will take our individual pleas to her son and help them to be answered as well.

John 2:1: 'On the third day a wedding took place at Cana in Galilee. Jesus' mother was there, and Jesus and his disciples had also been invited to the wedding.

When the wine was gone, Jesus' mother said to him, "They have no more wine."

"Dear woman, why do you involve me?" Jesus replied. "My time has not yet come."

Nearby stood six stone water jars, the kind used by the Jews for ceremonial washing, each holding from seventy-five to a hundred and fifteen litres.

Jesus said to the servants, "Fill the jars with water"; so they filled them to the brim.

Then he told them, "Now draw some out and take it to the master of the banquet."

They did so, and the master of the banquet tasted the water that had been turned into wine. He did not realise where it had come from, though the servants who had drawn the water knew.

Then he called the bridegroom aside and said, "Everyone brings out the choice wine first and then the cheaper wine after the guests have had too much to drink; but you have saved the best till now."

This, the first of his miraculous signs, Jesus performed at Cana in Galilee. He thus revealed his glory, and his disciples put their faith in him.'

So it's clear that Our Lady played a unique and essential role in the Son of God becoming incarnate in our world and her womb was an inviolate sanctuary protecting Jesus as he grew inside her, and so Mary is surely also a perfect model of motherhood for our world.

The Virgin Mary is also our spiritual mother, and ever since her assumption into Heaven she has performed an ongoing role as an intercessor for us to Jesus. Mary was entrusted with this role as a means of helping countless souls towards a deeper devotion of him and to help them along the path to eternal life.

The maternal love and compassion that Our Lady has for us was also clear in what she said to Juan Diego at Guadalupe in December 1531:

"I wish that a temple be erected here quickly, so that I may therein exhibit and give all my love, compassion, help, and protection, because I am your merciful mother, to you, and to all the inhabitants on this land and all the rest who love me, invoke and confide in me; listen there to their lamentations, and remedy all their miseries, afflictions and sorrows."

- Chapter 15 -

Our Lady's promise

When Our Lady appeared to the children for the second time, on the 13th of June 1917, she told Lucia about a devotion that Jesus wished to be established in the world.

"Jesus wishes to make use of you to make me known and loved. He wants to establish in the world devotion to my Immaculate Heart. I promise salvation to those who embrace it, and those souls will be loved by God like flowers placed by me to adorn his throne."

This was the first time that the request for this devotion had been mentioned by Our Lady, and Lucia also described having seen something else during this encounter:

"In front of the palm of Our Lady's right hand was a Heart encircled by thorns which pierced it. We understood that this was the Immaculate Heart of Mary, outraged by the sins of humanity, and seeking reparation."

At the third apparition, Our Lady said, "Sacrifice yourself for sinners, and say many times, especially when you make some sacrifice: 'O Jesus, it is for love of You, for the conversion of sinners, and in reparation for sins committed against the Immaculate Heart of Mary.'"

So here again, the need for reparation was expressed by Mary.

After having shown them the vision of Hell, Our Lady said:

"You have seen hell where the souls of poor sinners go. To save them, God wishes to establish in the world devotion to my Immaculate Heart. If what I say to you is done, many souls will be saved and there will be peace. The war is going to end; but if people do not cease offending God, a worse one will break out during the pontificate of Pius XI.

"When you see a night illumined by an unknown light, know that this is the great sign given you by God that He is about to punish the world for its crimes, by means of war, famine and persecutions of the Church and of the Holy Father. To prevent

this, I shall come to ask for the consecration of Russia to my Immaculate Heart, and the Communion of Reparation on the First Saturdays.

"If my requests are heeded, Russia will be converted, and there will be peace; if not, she will spread her errors throughout the world, causing wars and persecutions of the Church. The good will be martyred, the Holy Father will have much to suffer, various nations will be annihilated.

"In the end, my Immaculate Heart will triumph. The Holy Father will consecrate Russia to me, and she will be converted, and a period of peace will be granted to the world. In Portugal, the dogma of the faith will always be preserved .."'

So at the third apparition, Our Lady said that it was God who wished to establish this devotion to her Immaculate Heart and it was for the first time that she used the term 'Communion of Reparation on the First Saturdays.'

When Lucia was in her room at the Dorothean convent on the 10th of December 1925, Our Lady again appeared to her with the child Jesus, and here she showed Lucia a heart encircled by thorns which she held in her hand, and then Jesus said:

"Have compassion on the Heart of your Most Holy Mother, covered with thorns, with which ungrateful men pierce it at every moment, and there is no one to make an act of reparation to remove them."

Our Lady then said:

"Look, my daughter, at my Heart, surrounded with thorns with which ungrateful men pierce me at every moment by their blasphemies and ingratitude.

"You can at least try to console me and say that I promise to assist at the hour of death, with the graces necessary for salvation, all those who, for five consecutive months, shall confess, receive Holy Communion, recite five decades of the rosary, and keep me company for fifteen minutes while meditating on the fifteen mysteries of the rosary, with the intention of making reparation to me."

So here we have the specific details of how to make the devotion of the Communion of Reparation on the First Five Saturdays:

* **Attend confession.**

* **Receive Holy Communion.**

* **Recite 5 decades of the rosary.**

* **Spend 15 minutes meditating on the 15 mysteries of the rosary.**

The 15 minutes spent contemplating the mysteries is in addition to the reciting of the 5 decades of the rosary, and with all 4 elements of the devotion there has to be the intention of making reparation for the sins committed against her Immaculate Heart. The devotion has to be carried out on five consecutive first Saturdays of the month.

It's clear from the words used to describe the effect that these sins have on Our Lady that they are a source of great hurt to her and also that there's little respite from them as she said that the thorns of ungrateful men pierce her heart at every moment.

Jesus again appeared to Lucia two months later in the convent garden at Pontevedra on the 15th of February 1926, and He again spoke of this devotion:

"It is true, My daughter, that many souls begin, but few persevere to the very end, and those who persevere do it to receive the graces promised. The souls who make the five first Saturdays with fervor and to make reparation to the Heart of your Heavenly Mother, please Me more than those who make fifteen, but are lukewarm and indifferent."

The promise that Our Lady made is quite incredible as she will assist at the hour of death all those who have made the devotion with the graces that are necessary for their salvation.

Here is a very brief description of the mysteries of the rosary, and included are the Mysteries of Light, the Luminous Mysteries, which John Paul II announced in 2002.

Joyful Mysteries: The first of these is the **The Annunciation,** when the angel Gabriel appeared to Mary saying, "Greetings you who are highly favoured! The Lord is with you." Gabriel announced that Mary would conceive through the Holy Spirit and carry the Son of God in her womb, and he also revealed that her elderly relative, Elizabeth was six months pregnant. Elizabeth would give birth to John the Baptist, the last of the Old Testament prophets. Mary showed her great faith and trust in God when she responded by saying, "I am the Lord's servant. May it be to me as you have said."

The next mystery is **The Visitation**, when Mary made the arduous journey from Nazareth to a small town in Judea to stay with her relative Elizabeth for three months. The child in Elizabeth's womb jumped for joy at hearing Mary's voice and Elizabeth then said, "Blessed are you among women, and blessed is the child you will bear!" Our Lady then sang a song in praise of God, which we know today as The Magnificat. Mary lived here with her relative until shortly before Elizabeth gave birth to John the Baptist.

The next joyful mystery is **The Nativity**. Joseph and Mary travelled all the way from Nazareth to Bethlehem, a distance of about 156 kilometres under very difficult circumstances as Mary was about to give birth. After Mary gave birth, three (or possibly more) devotees of the religion of Zoroastrianism visited the Holy Family having travelled all the way from Persia to worship the Messiah.

They brought gold to signify the divinity and kingship of Jesus, as well as frankincense, the fragrant white resin which was burned as an offering to God and which signified the holiness of the child Jesus. They also presented him with myrrh, a spice derived from the resin of the myrrh tree, which was used in the embalming process. This gift was symbolic of suffering and was prophetic, as Jesus was offered the anaesthetising myrrh mixed with wine at his crucifixion, but he refused to drink it. Joseph of Arimathea and Nicodemus would later use myrrh and aloes to embalm the body of Jesus.

The 4th mystery is **The Presentation**. Eight days after his birth, Jesus was taken to the temple to be circumcised as required by Mosaic Law, and Mary and Joseph were met there by Simeon in the Temple Courts. It had been revealed to Simeon by the Holy Spirit that he wouldn't die until he'd seen the Christ of God. Simeon blessed Mary and Joseph, but he also cautioned Mary that a sword would pierce her soul, and this was one of the seven sorrows that she would have in her life.

The last of the joyful mysteries is **The Finding in the Temple**. Mary, Joseph, and the 12 year old Jesus went up to Jerusalem for the annual celebration of the Passover, but unknown to his parents, Jesus didn't join the caravan going back to Nazareth. They anxiously searched for him but only found Jesus three days later in the temple at Jerusalem, sitting with all the teachers of The Law. Luke wrote in his gospel: 'When his parents saw him, they were astonished. His mother said to him, "Son, why have you treated us like this? Your father and I have been anxiously searching for you."

"Why were you searching for me?" he asked. "Didn't you know I had to be in my Father's house?"' (Luke 2:48)

Sorrowful Mysteries: The first of these is **The Agony in the Garden**, which refers to the anguish that Jesus experienced in the olive grove called Gethsemane after the last supper. It was here that Jesus made the great act of faith that we can all imitate in times of difficulty or suffering: **"Father, if you are willing, take this cup from me; yet not my will, but yours be done."**

Jesus knew the terrible suffering that he was about to endure, and in this anxious state his sweat looked like blood as it fell to the ground according to Luke, who was a physician. This can happen under conditions of great stress when blood enters the capillaries of the sweat glands. Judas Iscariot soon arrived with the chief priests and a cohort of the Temple Guard and he then walked over to kiss Jesus on the cheek, prompting Jesus to ask, "Judas, are you betraying the Son of Man with a kiss?"

Peter drew his sword and struck out at Malchus, the servant of the High Priest, cutting off his right ear, and it was then that Jesus performed a miracle by healing him. Jesus was then taken to the house of Caiaphas where the Temple guards blindfolded and beat him, saying, "Prophesy to us, Christ! Who hit you?

Jesus was questioned by the Sanhedrin, and it was here that the High Priest asked him, **"Are you the Christ, the Son of the Blessed One?"** Jesus replied, **"I am. And you will see the Son of Man sitting at the right hand of the Mighty One and coming on the clouds of heaven."**

It was also here that Peter denied knowing Jesus three times just as Jesus had foretold at the Last Supper.

The 2nd sorrowful mystery is **The Scourging at the Pillar**. Jesus was taken to Pontius Pilate in the Praetorium to be questioned but the Roman Governor could find no fault in him at all despite all the charges brought against him by the Chief Priests. As Pilate was sitting on the judge's seat, his wife Claudia Procula sent him an urgent message saying, "Don't have anything to do with that innocent man, for I have suffered a great deal today in a dream because of him."

Pilate offered to have Jesus released but the crowd was whipped up by the Chief Priests to ask for a notorious criminal named Barabbas to be set free instead. Pilate then washed his hands, saying, "I am innocent of this man's blood," before having Jesus taken away to be flogged and crucified. Unlike the Jewish flogging of 40 lashes, which nearly always end up being 39, the Roman scourging was very brutal and had no limit on the number of strikes. In fact it was called a 'half death' because it was designed to bring the victims close to death so that they would spend less time hanging on their crosses.

The 3rd mystery is **The Crowning with Thorns**. The soldiers of the Praetorium dressed Jesus in a scarlet robe, placed a crown of thorns on his head and a staff in his hand, and then mocked him by kneeling on the ground, saying, "Hail, king of the Jews!" The soldiers beat Jesus on the head over and over again with a staff and spat on him, and after the beating they led Jesus off to begin his agonising walk along the Via Dolorosa to Calvary.

The 4th sorrowful mystery is **The Carrying of the Cross**. Jesus was led from the Praetorium carrying either the full cross or the beam of the cross called the patibulum, which would have weighed at least 35 kilograms. Jesus was so weakened from the beatings and the scourging that he stumbled and fell for the first time, and tradition tells us that it was then that he met his beloved mother.

The soldiers then forced Simon from Cyrene to carry the cross for the walk to Calvary and along the way a woman braved the hostile crowd and the soldiers to rush up to Jesus and hand him a towel (sudarium) with which to wipe the blood and sweat from his face. For this outpouring of love, Jesus rewarded her by leaving a miraculous imprint of his face on the towel. The real name of the woman is uncertain as Veronica is simply a fusion of the Latin words 'vera' for true, and 'icon' for image.

Jesus fell for a second time and it was then that he saw several of the women who'd helped him on his three year ministry and he turned and said to them, "Daughters of Jerusalem, do not weep for me; weep for yourselves and for your children." Jesus then fell for a third time before he finally reached the crucifixion site of Golgotha.

The last sorrowful mystery is **The Crucifixion**. Jesus was offered wine mixed with myrrh, but he refused to drink it, and he was then nailed to the cross by four guards, between two thieves named Dismas and Gestas. Jesus forgave the soldiers who were crucifying him, saying, **"Father, forgive them, for they do not know what they are doing."** This was the first of seven statements that Jesus made from the cross.

Pilate had a notice pinned to the cross which read 'King of the Jews', much to the anger of the chief priests who were standing there. The soldiers then cast lots for the undergarment of Jesus as had been prophesied by David in Psalm 22, written a thousand years earlier.

With the exception of John, all the gospel writers mention a three hour long period of darkness in the middle of the day beginning at the sixth hour, and so from about 12 o'clock midday until 3pm Jerusalem was pitch black.

From the sixth hour until the ninth hour darkness came over all the land. (Matthew 27:45)

It's significant that this darkness was not just described by the authors of the gospels but that it was also described by Tertullian in 'The Apologeticum' and he clearly did not believe that the phenomenon was caused by an eclipse.

He wrote in chapter 21: **'In the same hour, too, the light of day was withdrawn, when the sun at the very time was in his meridian blaze. Those who were not aware that this had been predicted about Christ, no doubt thought it an eclipse. You yourselves have the account of the world-portent still in your archives.'**

The Greek historian Phlegon also referred to this inexplicable darkness in his 'History of the Olympiads' which was written about 137 AD, stating that it was so dark that the stars could be seen. He wrote:

'In the fourth year of the 202nd Olympiad, there was an eclipse of the Sun which was greater than any known before and in the

sixth hour of the day it became night; so that stars appeared in the heaven ...'

The fourth year of the 202nd Olympiad ran from July 32 AD through to the end of June 33 AD.

Gestas mocked Jesus, as did the crowds walking past the cross, but Gestas was rebuked by Dismas who then turned to Jesus and said, "Jesus remember me when you come into your kingdom."

Jesus, as ever filled with compassion and mercy, replied, "**I tell you the truth, today you will be with me in paradise**."

Jesus saw his mother standing nearby with Mary Magdalene and Mary the wife of Clopas, and he said to his mother, "**Dear woman, here is your son**." He then said to the disciple John, "**Here is your mother**."

Mark wrote that it was at the ninth hour (3 pm) that Jesus uttered the words, "**Eloi, Eloi, Lama Sabachthani?**" meaning "**My God, My God, why have you forsaken me?**"

Jesus was fully divine and also human, and this anguished cry was made by Jesus the man, who was now at the point of death. Jesus then said, "**I am thirsty**," which prompted one of the bystanders to dip a sponge in vinegar, which he then held up on a hyssop stick for Jesus to drink.

After this, Jesus said, "**It is accomplished**."

Luke's Gospel is unique in that it records the last words of Jesus being, "**Father, into your hands I commit my spirit**."

Jesus died after hanging on the cross for 6 hours and immediately there was a major earthquake during which the curtain in the Temple of Jerusalem, which was 60 feet high and four inches thick, was torn in half thus exposing the 'Holy of Holies.' This section of the temple was reserved for the High Priest, who alone could enter it in order to offer up sacrifices for man's sins, but now that God's plan of establishing a new covenant with man had been accomplished, Jesus had become the everlasting sacrifice for our sins.

When the crowds who'd been mocking Jesus saw these staggering events, they walked away from Calvary beating their chests, and the pagan centurion Longinus, who was standing guard at the cross, said, "Surely this man was the Son of God!"

Longinus later thrust a lance into the side of Jesus, and immediately blood and water gushed forth from the wound. Tradition has it that Longinus, who suffered from poor eyesight, was sprayed in the face when he did this, and that he was instantly healed, so even in death, Jesus brought about a miraculous healing. This tradition also holds that Longinus converted to Christianity after having witnessed the incredible events at Calvary that day.

Jesus was taken down from the cross by Nicodemus and Joseph of Arimathea, and they used 34 kilograms of myrrh and aloes with strips of linen to embalm his body. Once they'd finished, the two men moved a large rock across the entrance of the tomb, and this was later sealed by the Roman guard of at least 4 soldiers who had been stationed there at the request of the Chief Priests.

Glorious Mysteries: The first of these is **The Resurrection**. There was another earthquake in Jerusalem on the Sunday morning, and the gospels state that an angel appeared and rolled back the massive stone which had been placed across the tomb. The terrified guards ran off to report what they'd witnessed to the chief priests because they were too scared to tell Pilate that the body had gone.

The tomb was found empty early that morning by Mary Magdalene, Mary the mother of James, Joanna, and some other women (according to Luke's gospel). Mary Magdalene was the first person to see and to talk to the resurrected Jesus, and she was the first to give witness of the resurrection to the apostles. It was for this reason that Saint Augustine of Hippo gave her the title, 'Apostle to the Apostles.'

On hearing Mary Magdalene's account, Peter and John then ran over to the burial site near Calvary and entered the tomb, where they both saw the strips of linen that had covered the head and body of Jesus. Jesus later appeared to the disciples in the upper room, and he ate in front of them, but Thomas wasn't present that day and he refused to believe that Jesus had risen from the dead.

One week later, Jesus appeared again and this time Thomas was present. Jesus asked him to put his finger in the holes in his hands and to put his hand into his side where the lance had entered, and he then said, "Stop doubting and believe."

The stunned Thomas could only utter that great declaration of faith, **"My Lord and my God!"**

Jesus then said, "Because you have seen me, you have believed; blessed are those who have not seen and yet have believed."

The 2nd mystery is **The Ascension**. Jesus appeared to his disciples for 40 days after the resurrection during which time he continued to teach them and he also ate with them on several occasions. Jesus was then taken up into Heaven in front of his disciples outside the town of Bethany, a few kilometres from Jerusalem, and it was in this town that his friends Martha, Mary and Lazarus lived.

As the apostles were staring up into the sky, two angels appeared who gave them an assurance that Jesus would one day return to earth in the same way that he had left.

The next glorious mystery is **The Descent of The Holy Spirit** at Pentecost. Ten days after the Ascension, the disciples were baptised by the Holy Spirit, who appeared as tongues of fire above their heads, and this was the baptism of fire that John the Baptist had spoken of by the River Jordan. A powerful wind blew around the house as this was happening which quickly drew the attention of a large crowd of people who converged on the building.

Peter then emerged and gave a speech, which all in the crowd understood despite the fact that they were from many different countries and spoke a variety of languages, and he urged them all to repent and to be baptised in the name of Jesus, and three thousand did so that day alone.

The 4th glorious mystery is **The Assumption** of Our Lady, referring to the tradition that Mary was assumed into Heaven, both body and soul, immediately after she had died. The Virgin Mary was conceived without sin and had lived her life without sin and so she was able to be taken directly into Heaven.

The last of the glorious mysteries is **The Coronation**, and the origin of this tradition can be found in **Revelation 12:1**: 'A great and wondrous sign appeared in heaven: a woman clothed with the sun, with the moon under her feet and a crown of twelve stars on her head.'

Mysteries of Light: The first of these is **The Baptism of Jesus** in the Jordan at the age of thirty by John the Baptist, who had called the Jews to a baptism of repentance for the forgiveness of sins. As soon as Jesus came up out of the water, John saw the sky being torn open and the Holy Spirit descended on Jesus in the form of a dove and the crowd heard the voice of God saying, "You are my Son, whom I love; with you I am well pleased."

It was immediately after his baptism that Jesus went into the wilderness to fast and to pray for forty days in order to prepare himself for his ministry and for his later passion, thus emulating what Moses had done on Mount Sinai before he was given the Decalogue by God.

The 2nd mystery is **The Wedding at Cana**, an event which Jesus attended with his mother but not his father, and it's thought that Joseph had died by this time. The hosts ran out of wine and so Mary brought this to the attention of her son, confident that he would work a miracle.

There were 6 stone jars on the property which held between 450 and 690 litres of water, which Jesus then converted into wine. The Eastern Orthodox Church holds that the bridegroom at this wedding was Simon the Zealot who would become one of the 12 apostles.

The 3rd mystery is **The Proclamation of God's Kingdom**, which refers to the three year public ministry of Jesus with his apostles. Jesus appointed 72 men to go out to all the towns ahead of him in order to prepare the way, and he worked an astonishing array of miracles including the feeding of the 5000 and the 4000 with just a few loaves of bread and some fish.

Jesus also raised at least three people from the dead, including the son of a poor widow from the town of Nain and the twelve-year-old daughter of Jairus, a synagogue ruler. But he worked arguably his greatest miracle when he raised Lazarus to life in the town of Bethany after he'd been dead for four days.

The 4th mystery of light is **The Transfiguration**, when Jesus revealed his glorious divine nature to Peter, James and John on a high mountain (possibly Mount Tabor) and Matthew wrote that his face 'shone like the sun.' Moses and Elijah then appeared and spoke with Jesus, and the voice of God was heard to say, "This is my Son, whom I love. Listen to him!'"

The transfiguration showed the three apostles the glorious state of a resurrected body, which all people who die in God's love will assume.

The final mystery is **The Institution of Holy Eucharist** at the Last Supper. Throughout his ministry, Jesus had often referred to himself as 'the Bread of Life' and an example of this is found in John's gospel.

John 6:47: "I am the bread of life. Your forefathers ate the manna in the desert, yet they died. But there is the bread that comes down from heaven, which a man may eat and not die. I am the living bread that comes down from heaven. If anyone eats of this bread, he will live forever. This bread is my flesh, which I will give for the life of the world."

Then the Jews began to argue sharply among themselves, "How can this man give us his flesh to eat?"

Jesus said to them, "I tell you the truth, unless you eat the flesh of the Son of Man and drink his blood, you have no life in you. Whoever eats my flesh and drinks my blood has eternal life, and I will raise him up at the last day."

Jesus waited until the last night before his arrest and passion to share this meal with his disciples as by doing this his words would be emblazoned in their minds forever.

Luke 22:19: And he took bread, gave thanks and broke it, and gave it to them, saying, "This is my body given for you; do this in remembrance of me."

Matthew 26:27: Then he took a cup, and when he had given thanks, he gave it to them, saying, "Drink from it, all of you. This is my blood of the covenant, which is poured out for many for the forgiveness of sins. I tell you, I will not drink from this fruit of the vine from now on until that day when I drink it anew with you in my Father's kingdom."

At Calvary, Jesus gave himself up as a sacrifice for our sins, and by doing so he put right the relationship between God and His creation which had been fractured through disobedience, thus clearing the way for us to enjoy eternal life in Heaven.

Lucia, Francisco, and Jacinta witnessed 6 apparitions at Fatima in 1917, at which Our Lady called on mankind to repent and to cease offending God through sin. It was a mother who cares for us deeply who asked for us to turn to prayer and to make the First Five Saturdays devotion. Mary also asked that Russia be consecrated to her Immaculate Heart, and she assured us that if these requests were met, then the world would enjoy peace, and that many souls would be saved.

John Paul II did ultimately consecrate Russia to Our Lady, but the world has since turned to ever greater sinfulness, and unfortunately the devotion that she called for has been virtually ignored.

Clearly, her warning at Fatima of the global consequences of sin wasn't only for that generation, and World War II was the chastisement for the sins prevalent at that time in history, so surely the offence we are causing God today is putting mankind at risk of a far greater chastisement than this.

It's part of our human nature to doubt the existence of things we cannot see, but if we ever doubt the apparitions and the prophecies of Our Lady at Fatima, we should remember these words of Jesus:

"Believe me when I say that I am in the Father and the Father is in me; or at least believe on the evidence of the miracles themselves." (John 14: 11)

The Miracle of the Sun was witnessed by about 70,000 people on 13th October 1917, and many academics and journalists gave written testimonies of the spectacular and terrifying event they saw that day.

It's interesting that another great miracle involving the sun occurred at the crucifixion of Jesus when the sky became pitch black for three hours from midday. The ancient historians, Phlegon and Tertullian, both described this phenomenon in their works, with Phlegon writing in his 'History of the Olympiads' in 137 AD, that it was so dark that the stars could be seen. This event couldn't possibly have been caused by a solar eclipse because the longest period of darkness that can be associated with a solar eclipse is 7 minutes and 31 seconds.

Our Lady also gave a prophecy that there would be 'a night illumined by an unknown light' as a warning that another terrible war was about to break out, and this sign was indeed witnessed across the whole of Europe and parts of the United States on 25th January 1938.

In 1917, Mary prophesied that Russia would spread her errors throughout the world and our history books show us the suffering caused by the spread of communist Russia. Our Lady also said that the pope would have much to suffer and there was an assassination attempt on John Paul II on 13th May 1981, the anniversary date of the first apparition at Fatima!

Another miraculous sign given to us is that when Jacinta Marto's remains were exhumed in 1935, her face was still completely incorrupt and un-decayed.

But we shouldn't be surprised by all these signs, as great miracles accompanied the apparitions of Our Lady at Guadalupe in December 1531, and Lourdes in 1858. When Bernadette's remains were exhumed for the third time, on 18th April 1925, the doctors were stunned at the state of preservation of her body, with Doctor Comte remarking that this was not a natural phenomenon. There have been over 7,000 claims of miraculous healings associated with Lourdes, and the Church has officially recognised 70 of them after the most rigorous investigation.

Although the world has not adopted the devotion that Mary asked for, it's never too late for us to respond to her call as individuals, and for those who do so she has left us the most beautiful promise imaginable.

"Look, my daughter, at my Heart, surrounded with thorns with which ungrateful men pierce me at every moment by their blasphemies and ingratitude. You can at least try to console me and say that I promise to assist at the hour of death, with the graces necessary for salvation, all those who, for five consecutive months, shall confess, receive Holy Communion, recite five decades of the rosary, and keep me company for fifteen minutes while meditating on the fifteen mysteries of the rosary, with the intention of making reparation to me."

Printed in Great Britain
by Amazon

54974246R00086